NATURAL HEALING
for Total Emotional Well-Being

Also by Dr. Ann Wildemann:

*Understanding and Managing
Child Behavior in the 90's*

Stress Relief for the Childcare Professional

*Sessions: A Self-Help Guide
Through Psychotherapy*

The Shrink Plan

THE HERBAL MEDICINE CABINET

NATURAL HEALING
for Total Emotional Well-Being

By Ann Wildemann, Ph.D.

Adams Media Corporation
Avon, Massachusetts

Copyright ©2002, Ann Patterson Wildemann.
All rights reserved. This book, or parts thereof, may not be
reproduced in any form without permission from the publisher;
exceptions are made for brief excerpts used in published reviews.

Published by
Adams Media Corporation
57 Littlefield Street, Avon, MA 02322 U.S.A.
www.adamsmedia.com

ISBN: 1-58062-599-1

Printed in Canada.

J I H G F E D C B A

Library of Congress Cataloging-in-Publication Data
Wildemann, Ann Patterson.
The herbal medicine cabinet : natural healing for total
emotional well-being / by Ann Patterson Wildemann.
p.   cm.
Includes bibliographical references and index.
ISBN 1-58062-599-1
1. Herbs—Therapeutic use. 2. Mental illness—
Alternative treatment. 3. Stress management. I. Title.

RC350.H47 W554   2002
615'.321—dc21   2001055206

This publication is designed to provide accurate and authoritative
information with regard to the subject matter covered. It is sold
with the understanding that the publisher is not engaged in
rendering professional medical advice. If assistance is required, the
services of a competent professional person should be sought.

*This book is available at quantity discounts for bulk purchases.
For information, call 1-800-872-5627.*

Warning:
I do not advocate, advise, or recommend the use of any alternative remedy for treatment of disease or other chronic illness in lieu of medical treatment.

The use of some herbal products may be contraindicated when combined with certain prescribed medications. As with any other pharmaceutical, appropriate dosages of herbal products may vary according to an individual's body weight, health, age, gender, the quality and purity of a manufacturer's product, and many other factors, both known and unknown. The use of some herbs may have side effects that can be dangerous to your health. As more people turn to alternative medicine, information about both benefits and dangers continues to accumulate. The decision to use alternative or homeopathic remedies, and to assume the risks involved, is yours, and yours alone.

While the healing properties found in plant life may indeed enhance the quality of our lives when used in conjunction with the miracles of modern science, they are not substitutes. You should continue to have regular medical checkups and, when you are sick, see a doctor. I do.

Dedication

To my wonderful children; I love you all so very much. You are the joy in my life, and I feel so privileged to be your Mom. You are each perfect in every way, and I adore you all!

Special Thank-You

I want to take this opportunity to personally thank the special people who made my life easier as I wrote this book. My wonderful children are a constant source of loving support and motivation in life. Everyone pitched in—Mark, Brian, and Nick lent their vast computer expertise, ran errands, kept me supplied with Hershey bars, and made me laugh. Ellen organized me and also contributed editorially.

With a little help from my friends, Cathy Spitzenberger, Claudia Gravier, and Jennifer Christensen, the book came together. As the deadline approached, Judge Frank Sullivan helped with the final push.

No book ever makes it to press without the

effort and sage advice from a great agent. Dupree Miller is the best.

And last but not least, I appreciate all of the kindness and editorial talent from my publisher—my gratitude to Gloria Jasperse and Laura MacLaughlin at Adams Media Corporation.

Thank you all so very much.

Contents

Serendipity / xiii

1. Roots / 1
2. Aromatherapy / 21
3. Anxiety / 33
4. Insomnia / 51
5. Stress / 63
6. Depression / 79
7. Fatigue / 103
8. Memory / 115
9. Sexuality / 125
10. Aging / 153
11. Pain / 173
12. Weight / 201
13. Eating Disorders / 223
14. Kids / 239
15. Conclusion / 253

Appendix / 263

Bibliography / 269

Index / 277

About the Author / 288

Serendipity

When I was a little girl, I had my share of bumps, bruises, and cuts, not to mention insect bites, poison ivy, rashes, colds, and other sundry vexations. At the slightest provocation, such as a wounded child, my dad would open his medicine cabinet, which contained a fabulous array of lotions, salves, herbs, and ointments. I remember the sweet aroma coming from the colorful jars and bottles as Dad applied his magic. My father was nothing if not pragmatic.

Dad was a child of the Depression era, when people had to make do, a wonderful man who achieved greatness in his life, but who also never forgot his extremely modest beginnings. My grandfather was a butcher, and my dad drove a team of horses to make deliveries. Irish folk remedies, handed down from generation to generation, and often influenced by contributions from Native Americans, supplemented the paucity of a physician's resources during this difficult period. None of this was lost on my father.

I cannot begin to tell you the number of mustard plasters and necklaces of garlic I donned growing up. Just to make certain the concoctions would really work, my dad never failed to mention to us (I guess in an attempt to both reassure and add authenticity to his claim) that his very own father used this very same stuff on all of his horses. To state the obvious, if it cured a horse, it would cure a kid. But his remedies did not end there. He was a firm believer in vitamins, herbs, and other supplements and, of course, he watched his diet. All of these things served him well.

My father was bigger than life to me, and I adored him. From his days as a football quarterback at Georgetown University to jumping behind enemy lines in Germany, serving his country as a Marine officer with the O.S.S., my dad did everything. After the war, he rounded up Nazi criminals and was the youngest prosecutor in the Nuremberg trials. When he came home, he helped to create the Department of Defense and served in the United States Congress, garnering many prestigious honors. One of his bills haunts me in a loving fashion: When tornadoes are imminent, the warning whistles are sounded for all to take cover. It is as if my dad is watching over us all.

My dad had chronic heart disease for almost thirty years, but with his never-say-die attitude and, I believe, some of his own personal cures, he lived a very active, productive life. He was only ill a few days before he died at the age of eighty. All of those herbs and supplements paid off.

I must confess that personally I prefer pizza and hot fudge sundaes to seaweed and rice cakes, despite my knowledge of the important of nutrition. But my less than honorable eating habits came to a halt one summer day eighteen years ago. It is interesting how life can change in a matter of moments. And so it did. My youngest son Nicholas was diagnosed with juvenile diabetes at the tender age of two. Nicholas is adopted, but I strongly believe that although he did not come from my body, we were meant to be mother and son. Spiritually bound forever, serendipity is God incognito, and I am humbled daily by His gift.

Sadly, there are no cures on the horizon for juvenile diabetes, but a healthy diet is a major part of the treament. Once again, I was thrust, unwittingly, into the sea of nutrition, vitamins, and herbs.

Nicholas is doing very well and has grown into a very fine, handsome young man. But finding a cure is my fondest desire. It is to that end that some of the profit from this book will be dedicated to juvenile diabetes research.

Chapter 1
Roots

As a child, I was told a story of how man and woman came to be. God made a garden called Eden, a paradise in which to live—lush and green and embroidered with flowers and plants of all kinds.

Whether you believe literally in the Garden of Eden or see it as a metaphor, the truth is that relief from pain and suffering is only a lovely plant or delicate flower away. And with this truth, suddenly *nature* becomes *nurture!*

Our appreciation of the awe of our creator is magnified a hundredfold when we gaze in utter reverence at our rain forests, our oceans, our mountains, our deserts. The bountiful gifts received today hearken back to a time before time. As man emerged from the darkness of the cave into the light of the world, he carried with him a suitcase. In it, he carried his genes. Locked inside his DNA were the keys ultimately not only to his survival, but to the development of humankind.

From our earliest beginnings, we learned how to think—at first, rather concretely, but later the skills of abstraction and synthesis occurred. We created advanced civilizations and expressed our feelings through art, poetry, and music.

But along the road there were bumps, ups and downs, detours and, seemingly, some dead ends. Just as there is a yin for a yang, homeostasis was punctuated relentlessly with the good and the bad. Primitive villages grew to towns and then to cities and now to metroplexes. The genes in this suitcase were gradually added to, deleted, or mixed through human contact. Environmental changes occurred, as well as social and interpersonal relationships. All of these factors led to great achievements and a better way of life, but—returning to the yin and the yang—it also led to disease, both physical and mental.

But our friend who had ventured forth from the dark began to look around for some help. Experiencing some of the same problems that we do today, he improvised in order to bring some relief from pain—hunting trauma, bites of all descriptions, and, I am sure, depression and anxiety.

Through trial and error, wandering the earth and comparing notes with others, a body of knowledge based on plants and herbs became the underpinning for the science of medicine.

Early healers, often referred to as medicine men or mystics, wielded their crude instruments, applied and administered their herbs and incantations. We can trace this intriguing history of medicine from the very early Egyptians, Greeks, Chinese, and Indians—peoples from all over the globe—to modern time.

About four thousand years ago, a Chinese emperor named Che'en Nung compiled a book on natural healing, describing the usage of three hundred plants and herbs. What is fascinating about his work is that some of these herbs are still used, not just by emperors but by physicians as well.

Close to this time period, the Egyptians were also recording their experiences with herbs. By around the sixteenth century B.C., they had amassed a collection of prescriptions and formulas written on a scroll twenty-two yards long and twelve inches wide. It is called the *Ebers Papyrus*. Building on these ancient texts, the Greeks and Romans contributed volumes from their own discoveries.

By the fourteenth century A.D., London was a commercial hub, and among the trading bargains were herbs and spices. Unfortunately, some of the plants were misidentified, and furthermore, standards had not been set regarding the quantity to be taken. Mistakes were made. In 1753, a scientist by the name of Carolus Linnaeus addressed this need and developed the binomial system of plant nomenclature. Appropriate identification, specific application, and measurements ushered in the science of pharmacology.

When we look at herbal medicine, there are two major schools to be referenced. Developed by ancient practitioners, both are still going strong to this day and gaining much popularity. The first school is Ayurvedic medicine, and the second is Chinese medicine. Volumes have been written on both, but for our purposes, a succinct review of their holistic philosophy and theory will do.

Ayurvedic Medicine

Ayurvedic medicine has often been called the science of life. It was developed in India perhaps some 5,000 years ago and is the oldest medical system that we know of. The term *ayurvedic* comes from the Sanskrit root of *ayuh,* which means "longevity," and *veda,* which means "knowledge." The Veda is one of the oldest writings in history.

Ayurvedic medicine teaches that the human body is a microcosm of the universe. Since the universe is the macrocosm, the way we begin to understand our bodies is through observations of the world around us. Good health is realized by balance between the two. All of us fall into one of three categories called *doshas.* A dosha can perhaps be defined as a personality. The three doshas are (1) *vata* (space and air), (2) *pitta* (fire and water), and (3) *kapha* (water and earth). Now, some of these combinations do overlap, but we each have one dosha that is fairly prominent and distinguishes us from others. Vata personalities are associated with alertness, movement, creativity, and erudition. Vata personalities also include enthusiasm and generosity, and these folks are usually thin and energetic.

The pitta personality distinguishes those who are doers. These are people who are competitive and aggressive. Pittas may be aggressive and energetic and at times even a little hot-tempered.

Kaphas tend to be very centered, caring individuals. They tend to be good humored, down-to-earth, and supportive. They are very steady and reliable and are often associated with very slow-moving and solid constitutions.

A balanced dosha is associated with good health. Your natural constitution, which is referred to as *prakriti,* is the balance between the three doshas. Prakriti is present at birth and predominates in our lives.

High in the Himalayas the early holy men handed down Hindu scriptures that guided one toward the path of spiritual life and fulfillment. The medical aspect and knowledge from these Hindu scriptures embraced wellness as alignment of the body, mind, and spirit. If you go to an Ayurvedic practitioner, be prepared to answer a variety of questions on your lifestyle including exercise, diet, how often you meditate, your interests, and your emotions. The focus is going to be on prevention; however, Ayurvedic practitioners do have remedies for many different ailments that are chronic in nature, metabolic, or stress-related.

A core belief held by these practitioners is that each of us is responsible for our own health, and so they ask you to become their partner in treatment. While a variety of treatments may be offered, there are two basic approaches to Ayurvedic medicine. The first is constitutional, and the second is therapeutic. Constitutional treatments are directly related to one's lifestyle. The entire focus of constitution treatment is prevention of illness. Yoga for the mind and spirit, specific breathing exercises, massage to re-establish your energy, and perhaps even herbal supplements are suggested.

Therapeutic treatments are specifically designed to help rid the body of impurities, and, since the basic belief is that all disease arises from the gastrointestinal tract, guess what some of their very favorite practices are? If you are thinking enemas and induced vomiting, you are right.

The contribution of Ayurvedic medicine to our knowledge of herbs has been substantial. Perhaps the greatest contributions, however, are not necessarily related to herbs but reinforcing the idea that our mind, body, and spirit need to be in harmony in order to practice a lifestyle that is healthy as well as happy.

Chinese Medicine

The second major school of influence is Chinese medicine. The varied healing techniques and philosophy are well documented and enjoy a growing following in our Western society. Herbal usage in the Chinese tradition has been so successful that several prestigious universities (such as the University of Miami in Florida) offer a degree that prepares students to become Chinese physicians.

A pharmacy in the Republic of China has been compared to a trip to the natural science museum. Animal, plant, and mineral products are found among the shelves of this drugstore. These products have been tested and used by the Chinese for centuries. Recognizing and understanding the possible benefits from this 5,000-year-old heritage will certainly offer choices for improving our health.

Looking back to the legacy of Chinese medicine, the Han dynasty created a guide *(The Treatise on Diseases Caused by Cold Factors)* that is still considered valuable and practical today. This is amazing if one considers that the Han dynasty ruled from 206 B.C. to A.D. 220. Not to be left out, the Ming dynasty (A.D.1368–1644) produced the materia medica manual describing 1,892 different types of medicine. Both books have been translated into many foreign languages and used for medicinal purposes in East Asia and throughout Europe.

Chinese medicine is anchored in the forces of nature—the yin and the yang. This polar principle is founded in the belief of balance and unity. From the tombs of the Han dynasty, we find writings from the Yellow Emperor explaining the theory of yin and yang. According to the Yellow Emperor, yin and yang are the foundation of the whole universe and are constantly impacting life and death. Yin is created from the forces of darkness, while yang is from the forces of light. Yin created earth and is represented by confusion and turmoil. Yang created Heaven and is reflected as peace and serenity. Illness is the consequence of an imbalance of yin and yang. An equilibrium of the body's flow of energy will produce health. Traditional Chinese medicine will search for the balance of yin and yang.

The Chinese believe all living things are intertwined and are placed on Earth for a reason. A human body in our universe is part of the same natural forces as the plants and flowers growing in the universe. Using the elements provided by nature for healing purposes is consistent with the belief in unity and balance. Medicine and healing is the search for harmony to restore balance in our universe.

The foundation of Chinese medicine in the human body is *qi* (pronounced "chee"). As the air, land, and sea creates nature, qi, blood, and moisture create the human body. The energy that allows our bodies to move and work and our minds to think, feel, and create is qi. It is the vital energy found in all living organisms.

In addition to the blood and fluid that circulates in the vascular system, muscles, bones, nerves, skin, and organs are part of the *xue* (blood) component of our body. Finally, *jin ye,* the liquid in our body, is moisture, which protects, lubricates, and nurtures our tissues. This includes tears, perspiration, saliva, milk, mucus, genital secretions, and hydrochloric acid. Jin represents the yang fluids, which are considered lighter and purer. The lung network uses the jin to moisten and nourish the skin and muscles. Ye, the yin fluids, are thicker; ye fluids are located in the stomach and spleen and used to moisturize and nourish the internal organs, brain, bones, and orifices.

In addition to qi, xue, and jin ye, *shen* and *jing* impact our balance of harmony. Shen is our spirit, how our nonphysical being is stated. It is our conscious condition of motivational, mental, and emotional energy. Jing is our essence, the physical body's ability to reproduce and rejuvenate. Jing is the energy we inherit from our family with the energy gained from our daily life. Chinese medicine recognizes the value and importance of these unseen forces as a part of our physiology.

Qi, xue, jing, shen, and jin ye are considered the five forms of qi energy. These five forces are interdependent, but qi is the principal activator. Qi has five dominant functions for the healthy flow of energy in our body: impulsing, warming, defending, controlling, and transforming. Creating a balance for the human qi is vital. As we are all part of the cosmic universe, everything we drink and eat impacts qi. The air we breathe is equally important, because the Chinese tradition holds that energy for the body is from the qi found in breathing and consumption. A person's health and lifespan is dependent on the amount, quality, and harmony of qi in your body.

Qi, xue, jin ye, shen, and jing are integral to a healthy body in harmony with the universe. The organ network of the liver, spleen, kidneys, lungs, and heart are dependent on the five energies. To begin with, the liver is in charge of storing blood, regulating the flow of qi, and tempering our constitution; it maintains our emotional response to actions in the external environment. The liver network includes the limbs and trunk of our body. Thus, the result of imbalance in these areas may result in shoulder and neck pain, high blood pressure, headaches, possible cramping, and irritability.

The spleen is recognized as controlling the flow of food and fluids. It directs the metabolism and the dispersion of nutrition throughout our body. Our strength, vigor, and physical body are deeply impacted by the functioning of the spleen network. In addition, it regulates a person's thoughts and ideas. Thus, disruption to the spleen network can affect concentration, precise thinking, and decision-making. Disorder may also result in fatigue, bloating, and indigestion.

According to Chinese beliefs, jing is stored in the kidneys, affecting our reproduction, growth, and rejuvenation. Our human life force is dependent on this network. The kidney system has a great amount of work regulating bones, marrow, teeth, inner ear, eye pupils, the lumbar region, and our brain. The kidneys are also responsible for our emotional feeling of fear, our free will, and critical thinking. The Chinese believe that dysfunction in the kidney system may be expressed as mental retardation, lower back pain, poor vision, ringing in the ears, and infertility. Indifference, depression, and obscured thinking may also be related to kidney network failure.

As we extract qi from the air we breathe, the lung creates our body's rhythm with each breath. It is our cybernetic balance. Additionally, the lung is responsible for inspirations and guarding our boundaries. Colds and influenzas are credited to a poor functioning lung system. Skin rashes, chest tightness, and gloominess are all thought to be a result of disharmony in the lung network.

Finally, the heart network shelters the shen and controls the mind. The heart system is the control center of our body represented by intelligence and consciousness. The Chinese recognize the function of the heart to move blood through the vessels as well. Heart disease and palpitations occur if the heart network is encumbered. Anxiety and insomnia may also plague our bodies if balance in this network is not found.

Because Chinese medicine sees each human body as its own ecosystem, diagnosis is derived from examining the energy found in the body. Feeling a person's pulse on their wrist and examining the color of the face, tongue, and body are the first steps to diagnosis. Information is also gathered from the person's physical living environment, history of family health, emotional status, lifestyle habits, work demeanor, and past and present complaints.

Treatment in traditional Chinese medicine is achieved in balancing a person's yin and yang. Harmony is accomplished by adjusting the qi, blood, moisture, and network of organs. Treatment may result in acupuncture, herbal remedies, change in diet, exercise, and massage. Duration of treatment is dependent on the individual progress of each patient.

Chinese medicine has become established over the years through the meticulous works of its practitioners. Historically, the Chinese have used themselves as the guinea pigs for testing new plants and establishing reliability of their science. Classifying the effects of different plants and minerals for correct dosage and usage has created the legacy of their work. Their understanding of the natural phenomena and the place of humans in this universe offer great advantages to increasing overall health and longevity of life.

What You Should Know

Depending upon whose research you use, herbal medicine accounts for treating the ills of many people. The World Health Organization believes that 80 percent of the world's population turn to herbs for their healthcare. Pharmaceutical houses depend on these plants, either directly or indirectly, as central ingredients for prescribed medications.

Americans are beginning to catch up with the popularity that herbs have enjoyed for some 4,000 years in Asia, India, and South America. Most prescriptions in Europe are written for herbs, but until the United States media focused on the significance and effectiveness of these plants, herbal usage was relatively overlooked. During the 1960s, some folks were experimenting (not scientifically, of course) with any plant they could find and inadvertently encouraged research in this area. During the 1970s and 1980s in the United States, there emerged an attitude of self-reliance and a recognition of the need to become more responsible for one's own health. The philosophy of alternative medicine, with its variety of methods, techniques, and herbal remedies, enticed consumers who were looking for noninvasive, less expensive, readily accessible cures. Journalists like Bill Moyers, through his programs on the Public Broadcasting System (PBS), educated many and made believers take a chance.

The "chance" paid off, and today it has been estimated that one out of every three of us spends well over $200 per year on herbal alternatives, making it a multibillion-dollar business. It is also one of the top five fastest growing industries, and for good reason—many of these herbal preparations work just as well as any synthetic drug. Once again, I must point out that you should always consult with your physician first before delving into the alternatives.

Apart from cost and availability, herbs offer another important advantage over synthetic drugs—side effects from herbs are rare if they are taken correctly. The downside with herbs is that they usually require a longer period of time to bring relief, and, since we are often impatient for results, a synthetic drug may be a quicker option.

Before you reach for an herb, there are some things you must be aware of in order to make an appropriate choice. The scientific community is making major advances in studying these plants, but a big drawback is the issue of standardization. Before we address the issue of standardization, however, you need to have some knowledge and background on how research and studies are done.

In order for a study to be of scientific merit and value, regardless of the subject matter—whether plants, animals, or humans—there are specific procedures, protocol, and criteria that must be met. The first test is *reliability,* which, among other things, seeks to answer the question, "Can we count on the results, reliably?" Reliability looks at the study's methodology to determine whether it is sound. The second test is *validity,* which asks the question, "Can the study be repeated and come out with the same conclusion?" Notice, we are not addressing whether the herb works, or its efficacy, or if it does what we hope it will do—only the examination *procedures.* When an herb is being tested, the scientist, based on past research previously compiled and analyzed, has an idea of its application in managing or curing a disease. What I have just briefly described are the rigors of scientific scrutiny, but what I am going to tell you next is where things can go wrong. Herbs are active biochemical compounds, and their safety and potency may vary with the particular raw material used and with the production process. Any given plant may differ from another depending upon growing conditions, the part of the plant that is cultivated and used, when the plant is harvested, its preparation and storage. Environmental factors must be considered as well throughout this entire process, such as air, moisture, and light. All of these variables fall under the category of "standardization," and, unfortunately, standardized practices are minimal and often not enforced.

The Food and Drug Administration (FDA), which oversees pharmaceutical products, does not have much regulatory control over supplements.

That is probably just as well since they are very slow to react, which, in turn, would cause the cost of producing herbal supplements to go through the roof. Currently, the only role of the FDA is to remove from the market any herb that is harmful or misidentified.

The federal government passed a bill in 1994 creating the Dietary Supplement Health and Education Act (or DSHEA). It allowed for greater accessibility of plants to consumers and outlined some general rules for manufacturers regarding labeling, including the description of how the plant may affect the body, which they refer to as "structure and function." As mentioned previously, the manufacturer is forbidden to describe what it is actually used for, so the average shopper is largely dependent on the knowledge of the clerk who sells it.

Most physicians and pharmacists have a dearth of knowledge when it comes to herbs, so self-education is important. Professionally trained herbalists, homeopaths, Chinese physicians, and some nutritionists may be other good resources. *But you must ask questions!* As you probably know, many herbs contain elements that render it useful for more than one problem. I cite the particular use of bilberry, a common, well-researched herb, that during the last trimester of pregnancy may be used to help prevent hemorrhoids. But unless you did the research, you may not be aware that it can also help treat diabetic retinopathy, herpes, fungus, and night blindness, all seemingly unrelated entities. The explanation for the diverse usage may be understood when you examine what part of the plant is being used (for example, the root or leaf), the method of administration (oral or topical), concentration, and dosage. Obviously, this is a very simplistic overview of a very complex situation.

Standardization is a vital issue when it comes to processing herbs for therapeutic use. This process ensures that therapeutic effects can be realized, that the appropriate levels of chemicals or compounds are contained in the product, and that purity, uniformity, and safe health production practices are followed.

Throughout my book, I will continually make reference to the *German Commission E Monograph*. You may think of this group as a form of our FDA, but without the FDA's bureaucracy and red-tape studies that may take five to ten years and cost billions of dollars. The efficient German government convenes a panel of experts consisting of scientists, physicians, pharmacologists, toxicologists, and even consumers to review research studies, clinical trials, and quality control by manufacturers. They then publish periodic reviews that evaluate the herb, taking into consideration its effectiveness, dose, side effects, and contraindications. Once the herb receives a positive review, it is labeled as "Commission E" and may then be sold over the counter. Several years ago, the *Commission E* was translated into English.

Just because an herb is packaged attractively does not guarantee standardization. The word "standardized" must be printed on the label. Also prominently displayed should be the herb's scientific name (in Latin) as well as its common name and what part of the plant was used. The dosage recommendations, expiration date, and name of the manufacturer should also appear. I will mention one other thing about the label because this usually appears close to it—the sticker that shows its cost. There is no way to make a decision regarding the quality of the herb based on how expensive or inexpensive it may be. Be more concerned about standardization than anything else. One other tip: It is better to use brands that are produced by large companies that have been in business for a long time.

Herbs can be purchased from a variety of places such as grocery stores, Chinese herb shops, health food stores, and pharmacies. They are all essentially over-the-counter sales, which gives you an opportunity to ask about the brand. Such questions as how long has this store been doing business with a particular manufacturer, what is the manufacturer's reputation, and even seeking a recommendation are all very legitimate inquiries.

Whether you prefer to take an herb as a solid (tablet or capsule) or liquid (tea or decoction) may be predicated on its use or convenience, but some general precautions should be considered. First, consider characteristics such as your age, weight, and health, and whether you are using any other herbs. Avoid mixing medications with herbs, and make certain that an herb will not interfere with any pre-existing medical conditions. Tell your family doctor what you are taking and if you are pregnant or breastfeeding—always, *always* consult your obstetrician and/or pediatrician. Finally, don't pick herbs that may grow wild and look prickly; it's not a good idea.

Most herbs are very safe and can provide relief for a myriad of problems. They are ideal home treatments and can be wonderfully gentle remedies as well as preventive medicine. Do a little reading, ask some questions, and you just might discover a very interesting subject.

After six thousand years, active ingredients from many plants are still contained in at least 25 percent of modern prescriptions. Interestingly, in Europe approximately 75 percent of all prescriptions written are for herbs.

Somewhere along the way, a tragedy occurred. We literally lost track of our "roots." The proliferation of scientific advances overshadowed some of the old tried-and-true natural aids. We stopped using the word "herb" and started using the word "drug," even though many of our "roots" were the precursors of today's pharmaceutical wonder drugs.

Behavioral Helpers

The emphasis in medicine today is on prevention, which squarely places our own choices center stage. Perhaps, another term for prevention could be "responsibility." We must take our lives into our own hands. We can do this through good nutrition, regular activity, and general healthy lifestyle patterns such as:

- Not smoking
- Appropriate weight maintenance and exercise
- Not abusing alcohol or drugs
- A balance between home, work, social life, and spirituality
- A positive attitude

Now, many of these suggestions people already know about and have put into practice, but mainstream usage of herbs is still in the embryonic stage in America. Our European cousins have used them for years, especially in Germany and France, with exciting results. Researchers are sharing their findings and enthusiasm, which tends to be contagious.

In the following chapters, I will be telling you more about specific herbs that may help you feel a lot better. But also, along the way, I want to share some "behavioral helpers" that can make a significant difference in how you deal with others and how you view yourself. Additional recommendations regarding aromatherapy and the research that supports its uses will be explained.

Chapter 2
Aromatherapy

Hand in hand with herbal therapy goes aromatherapy. Aromatherapy has been around a very long time, but until just recently it was, at best, ignored. Phrases like "I smell a rat" or "something is fishy" are obvious connections of our olfactory sense (smell) to the limbic system (emotion). Scents trigger emotion and serve as links that cue memories, good or bad.

Aromatherapy is a natural form of healing. One of the first senses that develops in newborns is the sense of smell, and those first memories stay with us most of our lives. The smell of apple pie or cookies baking in the oven is pleasing as we think back on our childhood and associate these lovely smell messages with the things that were pleasurable to us at different stages of our lives. Of course, there are always naysayers about any type of theory that seems to be brand new.

Scientists believe that there are approximately 5 million to 7 million nerve receptors in our nostrils that pick up different scents. When these nerve receptors are activated, they go directly to the brain and produce pleasure—or sometimes, displeasure.

Studies suggest that the connection takes place in the limbic system because it is the link between the olfactory nerves, the brain, and the sense of smell. Further adding to this connection is the association of the limbic system with memory and emotion. Researchers suggest that the smell that is processed through our body then impacts our behavior. Aromatherapy is introduced into our body through either our nose or our skin.

As you may remember from science or health class, the skin is the largest organ in the body and also has the ability to absorb aromas. During a massage, when essential oils are used, the body reacts pleasurably. Not only is your brain taking in the sense of feeling (the tactile sense), but it is also processing the sense of fragrant oils.

Essential oils, which are the basis for aromatherapy, can be found in a variety of interesting places ranging from plants to the bark of trees. Extracting the oil for use can be done quite creatively.

For example, sometimes people will press and release the essential oils from the leaves or stems themselves, or will distill it, using various methods, or they will heat the pod or leaf containing the oil to release its fragrance. Essential oils are usually colorless and highly concentrated. Using just a drop or two is effective in producing desired results. It takes many pounds of petals to make an ounce of oil and can be very costly. Only pure oil is therapeutic; synthetic products do not do the job.

Historically, the Egyptians used floral scents to entice and arouse, setting the groundwork for the pleasurable uses of aphrodisiacs. Apparently, Cleopatra knew what she was doing. Her ability to entice great leaders and have them do her bidding is a fascinating piece of history. It is believed that she was a true master of aromatherapy and had great factories in Egypt that produced wonderful scents. The Egyptians included these scents in their embalming process, known as mummification.

Suggesting that Cleopatra is responsible for making the whole world smell better might be fair. Travelers, who came to Egypt and experienced the pleasure derived from these aromas, took their treasures back to different parts of the world. The Romans and the Greeks utilized the fragrances as perfume but also used them in religious ceremonies and rituals and healing practices. Hippocrates was one of the first people to talk about the healing impact of scents.

Today, the research into human pheromones identifies smells that will attract the opposite sex. But that is just the tip of the iceberg. Science has proven that particular scents may activate neurotransmitters in the brain. The result can influence how we feel—stimulated or relaxed.

Even though aromatherapy is gaining more prominence in the United States, the scientific community has not embraced it. As a result, it is still considered an alternative to traditional Western medicine. Claims that it cures different illnesses and problems should probably be taken in a guarded fashion.

Our stressed-out lifestyles make people eager to embrace some of the simpler things in life, like smelling a plant or a flower. With the increased demands that we all face as members of a busy society, many people are looking for natural-type cures and answers to ease their burdens. Aromatherapists believe that essential oils are truly miraculous. A word of caution: essential oils can be toxic, as they are highly concentrated essences of plants.

Herbs for Your Nerves

The following is a list of essential oils and their uses in aromatherapy:

◄ Angelica ►

An earthy and sweet aromatic, angelica is used to provide pain relief and to stimulate the immune system. The scent is inhaled to treat dizziness, nausea, and anxiety. It is used to help with chest congestion, colds, and bronchitis. It may relieve pain from headaches and mild toothaches. Applied topically, angelica can be helpful in healing skin irritations, cuts, bruises, and psoriasis. Use of angelica root oil should be avoided when sunbathing, as there is some evidence that the oil is phototoxic.

Atlas Cedarwood

Smelling somewhat like dry wood mixed with turpentine, this oil is distilled from a large evergreen tree common to the Atlas Mountains of Algeria. It is used as a decongestant and expectorant but should not be taken internally. Applied to the skin, Atlas cedarwood has been used for treatment of acne, dandruff, dermatitis, oily skin, and fungal infections. The wood is burned in Tibetan temples as an incense to aid in meditation. Best avoided during pregnancy, the oil is nontoxic and is sometimes used to stimulate hair growth.

Bergamot

When inhaled, the spicy scent of bergamot acts as an antidepressant and may be used for treatment of respiratory problems. Moderately applied topically, it limits activity of the herpes simplex and zoster viruses, and it's a good insect repellant. Excessive application to the skin may increase photosensitivity or irritate sensitive skin.

Taken internally, bergamot may be helpful in treating indigestion.

◄ Blue Gum Eucalyptus ►

Used in many modern pharmaceutical products, eucalyptus has numerous healing properties. When applied to the skin, the diluted oil acts as an antibacterial agent useful in treating wounds, burns, and other skin conditions, including herpes blisters. Aborigines of Australia have been known to apply crushed leaves directly to wounds to fight infection, promote healing, and relieve pain. With citronella as an active chemical constituent, it is an effective insect repellant, especially when mixed with bergamot. Some use it to remove tar from clothing and skin. Frequently contained as an ingredient in commercial cold-care chest rubs, it acts as a good decongestant when inhaled. Dried eucalyptus is frequently used as a room fragrance. Eucalyptus should not be used by anyone with high blood pressure or epilepsy, and it may irritate the skin if used in large quantities.

◄ Clary Sage ►

Taken internally, clary sage is a sedative that can be very helpful to those experiencing premenstrual stress, cramps, backache, and muscle spasms. Taken in small amounts, clary sage oil is a euphoric, but may cause drowsiness in larger doses. It may be useful for treatment of digestive problems, including flatulence. It should not be used before or during driving or in any combination with alcohol.

◄ Frankincense ►

The long-lasting, rich aroma of frankincense has been used as an inhalant to clear lungs and nasal passages, ease shortness of breath, and promote respiratory function. As an aid to medication, the scent has a soothing, spiritually elevating effect on the mind. When burned, a consciousness-expanding chemical is released. Asthma sufferers may find that inhalation of frankincense oil calms the anxiety of an attack. It is often used in bathwater during menstruation for its cleansing, aromatic, and soothing attributes.

◄ Lime ►

Once carried on English ships to prevent scurvy (the origin of the nickname "limey"), this common fruit has antimicrobial and bactericidal properties that ease digestion, nausea, and upset stomach. As an aromatic, it eases cold symptoms including cough, sore throat, and congestion. It is frequently blended with angelica, eucalyptus, Roman chamomile, rose, and ylang-ylang to produce a pleasant, stimulating scent for relief of anxiety and depression. Applied topically, lime oil is a toning astringent for those with oily, but nonsensitive, skin conditions.

◄ Neroli ►

Made from the flowers of the "bitter orange tree," neroli is often applied directly to the dry skin to regenerate cells and improve elasticity. A natural tranquilizer when inhaled, the euphoric aroma may relieve anxiety associated with premenstrual stress and promotes restful sleep. Taken internally, it is antispasmodic and may aid in the treatment of diarrhea. Made solely from the flowering blossom, neroli is but one of three oils extracted from the orange tree. "Pure" orange is made from the fruit and pettigrain from the leaves.

◄ Niaouli ►

Possessing strong antiseptic qualities, niaouli is used commercially as an ingredient in some toothpastes and mouthwashes. It has been used as a water purifier and is good for the treatment of intestinal infections and parasites. When inhaled, it acts as a decongestant for those suffering from cold and other flu-like symptoms. Applied topically, the oil promotes healing of burns and is often used by radiologists to protect patients undergoing radiation therapy. It may be helpful in the treatment of acne, cuts, and insect bites. Some who live in the Middle East drink niaouli as a tea.

◄ Patchouli ►

Used medicinally in the Far East for treatment of headaches, cold, and gastrointestinal upset, patchouli is best known for its use in the 1960s as a body perfume. Because the oil possesses antiseptic and antimicrobial properties, it may be used to help healing of fungal infections, acne, eczema, and dandruff. Patchouli's strong, spicy aroma diminishes appetite when inhaled and tightens loose skin when applied topically. Taken internally, it is a natural diuretic.

◄ Roman Chamomile ►

Known since ancient times for its healing power, chamomile has a strong but fruity aroma. Ancient Egyptians considered the plant sacred and dedicated it to their sun god, Ra. It has been used to alleviate muscle pain, arthritis, and for the treatment of toothaches and headaches. Applied via compress, chamomile relieves pain associated with blisters, sprains, and inflamed joints. It has been used for treatment of acne, athlete's foot, and to relieve the pain of herpes outbreaks. As a relaxant, the aroma promotes feelings of well-being and may be beneficial for use by victims of insomnia or premenstrual stress.

◄ Rosewood ►

Distilled from the heartwood chippings, rosewood oil is relaxing, but not sedative. It has a sweet, spicy floral scent and has been used as an insect repellant and deodorant. Applied to the skin, it is beneficial for treatment of minor cuts, acne, scars, and wrinkles. As an aphrodisiac, it restores the libido by relieving tension and stress without drowsiness. It may help the body fight colds or other minor infections and relieves nauseous headaches.

◄ Sandalwood ►

Sandalwood is used so extensively in Asia that trees are now farmed exclusively for production of the oil. A strong aromatic, sandalwood has been used for thousands of years to aid meditation, relieve anxiety, and act as an aphrodisiac. When applied directly to the skin, it is an anti-inflammatory that relieves itching, dandruff, boils, and acne. It is said that a "dab" of the oil applied externally to swollen lymph glands will ease the pain of a sore throat.

◄ Yarrow ►

Possessing a sweet and spicy aroma, the flowering yarrow is used for hormone balancing and as a revitalizing tonic for the nervous system. It may act as an anti-inflammatory, anti-rheumatic, antiseptic, antispasmodic, diuretic expectorant, and stimulant. Mildly high blood pressure may be normalized with its use. It acts on the bone marrow and stimulates corpuscle replacement. It has been used for help with varicose veins and other circulatory disorders. Yarrow may relieve diarrhea, flatulence, or cramps. When applied to the skin, the plant encourages perspiration by opening the sweat glands, aids in healing minor cuts and rashes, and has even been used to promote hair growth. Excessive use may cause headaches and irritate the skin of some individuals.

◄ Ylang-Ylang ►

Derived from what is also called "the perfume tree," ylang-ylang oil is floral and has multiple uses. This potent oil has even been used for treatment of malaria. Women in the Pacific regions use a blend of the ylang-ylang and coconut oils as body moisturizers. However, ylang-ylang should not be applied to skin that is inflamed or affected by dermatitis. A powerful and euphoric relaxant, it has been used to calm panic, anxiety, excitement, and hysteria. Sniffed directly from the bottle, it is often used as a "smelling salt." In Indonesia, it is used on the wedding bed as an aphrodisiac and to relieve anxiety.

Remember: Never use more than two or three herbs at a time and *always* check it out with your family doctor first.

Chapter 3
Anxiety

Don't look back. Something may be gaining on you.
—*LeRoy (Satchel) Paige*

I once had a patient who came to my office complaining of anxiety. She didn't use that word, but her symptoms were a giveaway. All through childhood she would experience "jittery" feelings that only seemed to escalate. The more she thought about her jitters, the more she would feel them. If she felt a breeze blowing, she would then begin to fear a storm on the horizon, and the more she worried about the storm, her mind would reel to thoughts of a hurricane. Soon she would become totally out of control and consumed with fear. Her breathing would become rapid, and she would feel dizzy. All that she could focus on was impending doom.

Her behavior summarizes anxiety. Following are the classic symptoms:

- Palpitations
- Dizziness
- Sweating
- Trembling
- Irrational fear
- Nervousness
- Shaky hands
- Thinking about "what if"
- Headache
- Back or shoulder pain
- Nausea
- Muscle tightness
- Difficulty concentrating
- Irritability
- Fatigue
- Disturbed or interrupted sleep
- Insomnia

These are more subtle, chronic symptoms of anxiety:

- Worry over finances and the economy
- Obsessive thoughts

- Engaging in rituals
- Vulnerability
- Fear of rejection
- Guilt
- Shame
- Feeling unlovable
- Failure
- Hypochondria

But of course when you take a closer look, there is no storm; there is no hurricane. She was *catastrophizing.* She quite literally talked herself into a major anxiety attack.

Each year, approximately 65 million Americans will experience anxiety in one form or another, and those experiences will vary in frequency. Half of all sufferers are women, but since women tend to be more open about psychological discomfort, this may not be an entirely accurate figure. Unfortunately, of the folks who do suffer from anxiety, less than 25 percent receive any medical attention. Men are more likely to label anxiety as "stress," but regardless of what you call it, anxiety, untreated, makes you feel miserable.

A second type of anxiety is one in which the primary feeling of anxiety comes and goes and is seemingly triggered by some event. This can be very painful, and because it goes unannounced, patients feel that they are held hostage. Sometimes people will talk about feeling "worried," but if the worry is accompanied by restlessness, fatigue, muscle tension, or any other of three combinations from the symptom list, then we are really talking about anxiety—or, more specifically, an anxiety disorder. Some people have some symptoms of anxiety all of their lives and usually come from families where "worry" abounds.

Anxiety is a painful reaction to internal conflict. It differs from fear because fear is a response to an external threat. Fear is something that definitely exists—for example, really coming face to face with a hurricane.

Almost all of us have experienced anxiety at one time or another. There is some discussion in the literature regarding a genetic predisposition to anxiety, but this theory is relatively unsubstantiated. We tend to think that anxiety is a response to stress, unresolved childhood conflicts, or a learned behavior, but here is what we think happens on a biochemical level.

Deep inside the brain lies the amygdala, whose primary function is to send a signal to the cerebral cortex at impending doom. You can think of the cortex as sort of the "brains" of the brain. Upon receiving notice of alarm from the amygdala, the cortex makes a decision whether the threat is real or not. The problem, however, is this: The amygdala stores all negative memories and traumas, so even at the slightest inkling of a problem, it swings into action and immediately notifies the cortex. Any of the senses can set it off—a smell, a sound, etc. You may have forgotten the negatives, but your amygdala has not. The result, of course, is anxiety. Regardless of the cause, anxiety is very uncomfortable.

Children express anxiety in different ways than do adults. Some typical complaints from children experiencing anxiety might be:

- Overly concerned about performance
- Concern about grades
- Perfectionism
- Rigid need to conform
- Headaches
- Nausea
- Fear of earthquakes or nuclear disasters
- Checking and rechecking homework
- Tearfulness
- Night terrors

An anxiety disorder can lead to panic. Panic attacks have a sudden onset and usually last no more than ten minutes. But during those ten minutes, intense feelings occur. Patients have told me that they feel as if they are "going to die." The following symptoms during a panic attack explain those feelings:

- Rapid heart palpitations
- Sweating
- Difficulty breathing
- Hyperventilation

- Chest pain
- Feelings of choking
- Feelings of unreality
- Thinking that you are going crazy

Unpleasant as it might be, walking around feeling a little anxiety now and then is manageable, but when out of the blue you feel that you are dying is quite another. It is this sudden, unpredictable onset of severe symptoms that usually grabs someone's attention and leads them to seek treatment. One patient told me that during such an episode he had to pull over to the side of the road and stop the car and just "ride it out." More often than not, it is an emergency-room physician who makes the diagnosis of panic disorder.

Experiencing anxiety or panic does not mean that you are mentally ill or that you are having a psychotic episode. But it does mean that something is going on that warrants attention. Anxiety is often associated with low self-esteem—for example, people who doubt themselves or second-guess their decisions. Sometimes anxiety is related to an overactive superego, where a person becomes a slave to his or her conscience. Always motivated to do the "right thing," they cannot enjoy life and continually punish themselves. Parents who demand excessively high standards that are almost impossible to achieve create an atmosphere of tension and worry that carries into their children's adulthood. Over the years, I have treated many people who are extremely moral, but their religiosity induces guilt, fear, and honors suffering. Struggling with the concept that there is a big difference between a thought and the deed, anxiety becomes almost a defense mechanism. Any thought that one might have, no matter how horrible or disgusting, is okay. Only when one takes action on a thought and commits a crime, or does something wrong or inappropriate, is there a problem.

Guilt and anxiety have much in common. The good news is that they keep us on the straight and narrow. The bad news is that in the process, you can feel pretty lousy. Intrusive thoughts that are often embarrassing or create feelings of shame are characteristic symptoms of anxiety. Such thoughts assault your self-esteem and need to be challenged for accuracy. Another symptom in disguise of anxiety is obsessive thoughts or rituals. For example, if you continually question whether you are a good person, or are doing the right thing, that is obsessive thinking. People who need to check "just one more time" to see whether they turned off the stove or curling iron or locked all of the doors are exemplifying obsessive behaviors or rituals. It can be argued that they are just being careful and to some degree, I would concur. I would smile, but I would concur. But when intrusive thoughts become frequent, or obsessive behaviors begin to take over your life, it's time to get some professional help.

Periodic, mild feelings of anxiety or mild quirky

behaviors related to safety that do not interfere with normal life are acceptable. The key here is that if your normal life routine and that of those around you is relatively uninterrupted, you are just fine. But when you frequently experience anxiety in any form, or other people bring it to your attention, it's time to talk to a professional.

Fundamental to all anxiety is the belief that you are not in control. The truth is that we are always in control—even in the face of disaster. The actions and choices that you make are what keep you in control. It is only when we relinquish our personal power that anxiety rears its ugly head. Our mind and body speak to us through the language of symptoms. When your mind and body cause pain, fear, anxiety, or any other symptom, it is a signal to pay attention.

Anxiety is like a chameleon, changing symptoms to suit its purposes. As we have discussed, sometimes it comes in the form of worry, or fear, sometimes we can label it obsessional or ritualistic, but a less recognized form has to do with intimacy. If you think about it, I am sure that you can name at least one friend or couple who have been "engaged" or going together for five, maybe even ten, years. They love each other, but one of them just cannot, for seemingly no good reason, commit to marriage. Look back at the list of symptoms at the beginning of this chapter, and you will know the answer.

Another version of "intimacy anxiety" is the

person who can never be pleased. They find something wrong with everything and everyone. The real issue is that they find something wrong with themselves. Anxiety rears its ugly head. In order to love and be loved, you must take a risk. But risks can be painful, and anxiety seems to be a better choice. Unfortunately, it can be a very lonely choice.

An extreme form of anxiety is called agoraphobia and may or may not include symptoms associated with a panic disorder. The essential feature is characterized by a fear of being in places or situations from which there is no escape. Examples include anxiety about leaving home or traveling in a plane or train. This type of anxiety is very debilitating as one must plan one's life around this pervasive disorder. The anxiety impacts every part of life, from work, to grocery shopping, to driving, and may lead to the individual being a prisoner in his or her own home.

Agoraphobia should not be confused with social anxiety. Social anxiety is a persistent fear of social performance situations that may lead to embarrassment. People with social anxiety avoid others because they fear they are being judged. People with agoraphobia usually express anxiety about being alone. They do not feel safe in crowds, but they do like company.

Behavioral Helpers

Understanding the reasons behind the anxiety disorder is very important. We cannot medicate our emotions, but being able to calm the symptoms can be helpful while beginning the process of introspection. If the root cause of your anxiety is unresolved childhood conflicts, psychotherapy is just what the doctor ordered. Some things just need to be expressed and discussed. Internal struggles that perhaps are misunderstood, but cause pain and anxiety, can be relieved through a one-on-one open dialogue with a professional. Personal growth emerges from a search from within and an exploration of your belief systems and whether they serve you well or not. This is a form of mental housecleaning, sorting through and weeding out. It demands courage, this business of getting to the bottom of things, and at first may even create more anxiety. But self-examination, in the end, is very rewarding.

Sometimes we are so overwhelmed that we forget to take time out for ourselves—just to be quiet, to turn off that inner voice that has become familiar to so many of us. Learning how to relax is a wonderful therapeutic tool and can be easily learned. Relaxation is one of the greatest gifts you can give to yourself and will last a lifetime. It is an integral part of the treatment for anxiety. But for some quick, immediate help, I suggest the following deep breathing and mini-relaxer techniques.

Belly Breathing (Deep Breathing)

"Belly Breathing" is a wonderful technique that can be used anywhere and brings quick relief.

1. Sit or stand very erect.
2. Place two hands on your belly near your umbilicus (belly button).
3. Breathe in, allowing the air to expand your belly—pushing your hands out. *You should look a little pregnant.*
4. As you exhale, do it with a cleansing sigh, and visualize the tension being blown out of your body.
5. Repeat this belly breathing procedure at least four times.

Your breathing should be:

- Deep
- Rhythmic
- Belly inflating
- Exhaled with a sigh and image

Basic Mini-Relaxer Formula

1. Sit down in a quiet place, preferably a spot where you will not be interrupted or distracted. Once you become proficient, you can do it standing up in a large crowd of people!
2. Close your eyes and picture in your mind a very pleasant scene, for example, the lovely beach or majestic mountains that you have visited or seen in pictures.

3. Let your shoulders relax and perhaps even slouch.
4. Feel how heavy your eyebrows are, as you concentrate on your scenery.
5. Step into the scene. If you are at the beach, smell the salt air, hear the sea gulls calling, watch the gentle waves, feel the sun on your skin, touch the lovely white sand.
6. Hold on to that scene for several moments.
7. Slowly, take some deep, cleansing breaths and then gently come back.
8. Open your eyes and feel the relaxation.

The more you practice this basic technique, the more proficient you will become and the more you will benefit from the feeling of relaxation.

Practice . . . practice . . . practice!

Sometimes, you may wish to visualize a treasured moment or event, such as your first kiss or an experience with a friend. Just remember to:

1. See it (visualize it).
2. Listen to it.
3. Try to taste it.
4. Try to feel it.
5. Smell it.

One great way to deal with anxiety is to relax in a hot herbal bath to which you add a few drops of oil such as natural vanilla or rose. Keeping potpourri in either of these two aromas in your room will also aid in keeping you calm and peaceful.

Cognitive therapy is widely used to help people cope with anxiety, especially if the anxiety seems to be rooted in learned behavior. The essential goal is to have people rethink, in a positive fashion, their attitudes and beliefs. You are probably familiar with the example of seeing a glass half full rather than half empty. Processing life with an upbeat, happy, and positive outlook is far more beneficial than the opposite and is a skill that can actually be learned. People tend to get into ruts—not only doing the same old thing, but also thinking in the same old way. When you find yourself being critical, complaining about even the smallest of life's details, I promise you that you will be fostering and encouraging anxious feelings.

One form of behavioral therapy consists of systematic desensitization, where the patient gradually overcomes their anxiety by literally facing their fears. For example, if you have a fear of dogs, you will go through a specifically designed process of first just discussing dogs. When you are comfortable with that, you may be presented with a picture of a puppy. Once you can look at the picture without anxiety, then you may be shown a picture of an adult dog. Then you may be asked to listen to a dog bark, and after a few more treatments that escalate in intensity, you will upon "graduation" actually pet or even walk a dog. The technique is slow and nonthreatening and culminates with the absence of anxiety.

A technique (similar to the one I just described) that I often use in my practice is "worse case scenario." I see many people who become very anxious when called upon to speak or do a presentation. This is a very serious concern as their livelihood may be on the line. Using a hierarchical structure, I ask them questions that begin with very simple steps such as: "How do you feel when you are walking into the conference room? What is the worst thing that could happen?" Depending on their answer, I then ask them: "How likely is this to happen?" Next, we talk about how to avoid this occurrence. Gradually, they begin to recognize that *the* very worst thing that could happen is probably losing their job. With solid preparation, this is unlikely, but even if it did happen, we look at other opportunities. Succinctly put, their level of anxiety diminishes proportionately to the increases in their level of preparation and confidence.

Remember, anxiety is about losing control. Short of death, nothing is the end of the world. You are always in control.

Chromotherapy

The study of color and its impact on your mood and perhaps your health is called chromotherapy. If you are feeling anxiety, perhaps you may want to check your environment. Businesses, corporations, hospitals, schools, and advertisers all have a vested interest in what researchers have concluded regarding the way color can make us feel. According to some studies, color has the ability to stimulate the pituitary and pineal glands, which in turn influence hormonal changes and thus modulate emotional responses.

Most people are familiar with such expressions as "green with envy," "feeling blue," or "seeing red," but probably have dismissed the significance of these casual phrases. Big business, on the other hand, has paid attention. They understand the relationship between your emotions and the colors that may lend a hand in producing them.

So here it is, in black and white, what the "color experts" have to say:

- **Red** is the color of excitement and brightens your mood. It stimulates the nervous system and you!
- **Blue** reduces the rate of respiration and can be restful, calming, and act as a destresser.
- **Green** is tranquilizing, soothing, and may promote self-esteem.
- **Yellow** is happy, cheerful, and invigorating.
- **Orange** is touted to be the most energizing of colors and great for depression and fatigue.

The basic rule of thumb is that soft warm colors (pastels) such as peach, tan, and even orange, are peaceful; soft cool colors such as green and blue (brights) are energizing.

Interestingly, automobile manufacturers will tell you that black, white, or red cars make the best sale and have the best resale value. Jewelers echo this sentiment, suggesting that diamonds (white) and rubies (red) are the most popular gems.

Herbs for Your Nerves

◄ Valerian ►

Valerian is an amazing little herb whose ability to help relax the patient is well documented. This lovely perennial grows along riverbanks in Europe, and extracts of valerian root have long been a wonderful natural tranquilizer. Unlike a class of drugs known as benzodiazapines, such as Xanax and Valium, valerian helps with anxiety without the risk of addiction and serious side effects. This herb works much like the benzodiazapines on nerve receptors in the brain and creates mild sedation vis-à-vis the central nervous system.

Because valerian calms without drowsiness, it can be safely taken during the day. The recommended dosage for anxiety ranges from 150 milligrams to 300 milligrams. You can divide the dose according to your discomfort level and safely use up to 600 milligrams a day.

Remember that any time you are using an herb or any medication for anxiety, you are only treating the symptoms. Valerian should be thought of as adjunctive therapy, something to get you over the hump, but certainly not a total answer to the anxiety you are experiencing. Anxiety can get out of control and become very debilitating. In its more severe forms, panic attacks or agoraphobia, it requires professional attention.

Valerian should not be used without consulting your physician if you are taking other tranquilizers or antidepressants. Europeans have widely used this herb for years, and it is considered a safe and effective form of treatment for anxiety. It may be taken, day or night, but with a reduced dose during the day. The latest edition of the *German Commission E Monograph,* a text on herbal medicine, does not list any side effects, but one should always be a bit cautious.

◄ California Poppy ►

California poppy or *Eschscholtzia californica* was first discovered by a Russian physician and was so named. Leave it to Californians to find a legal form of opium. Obviously, it is quite different from opiates but comes from the same family.

California poppy is nonaddictive, and studies suggest that it is quite effective in reducing anxiety. This anti-anxiety agent can be used as a sleeping aid and, reportedly, is effective in stress reduction as well. Thus far, it is not in capsule form, and the liquid is very bitter to the taste, so you need to mix it with some type of fruit juice. As with all liquid extracts, you need to follow the directions because the strengths can vary. The recommended dosage is thirty drops with a glass of California orange juice!

◄ Passion Flower ►

Passion flower is another excellent choice. Native Americans used this herb to calm nerves and help with insomnia. The flower is white with a touch of blue, and early explorers gave it its name because the petals, stem, and leaves reminded them of the Passion of Christ. It grows wild in North America and South America and is the state flower of Tennessee.

Passion flower is a nonaddictive substitute for other prescription tranquilizers and can help wean people from the benzodiazapines. The recommended dosage is a half to one teaspoon of the dried herb to one cup of boiling water, and it can be taken every three to four hours. As a fluid extract, take three to four drops every four hours.

Remember: Never use more than two or three herbs at a time, and *always* check it out with your family doctor first. Herbs can be very helpful if taken correctly and in the proper dosages.

Chapter 4
Insomnia

To sleep: perchance to dream . . .
For in that sleep of death what dreams may come
When we have shuffled off this mortal coil,
Must give us pause.
                    —*William Shakespeare,* Hamlet III:1

There is a reason why infomercials are played in the wee small hours of the morning. It is because lots of Americans wrestle with the difficult problem of sleepless nights—or insomnia. Tossing and turning in bed and dreading the sun going up are complaints I hear from patients not infrequently. Our fast-paced society does not always allow problems to be worked out during the day; instead, those problems tend to keep us up at night. Approximately 75 million people suffer from insomnia and many have problems with anxiety—they seem to go hand in hand. It is one of the most common complaints that doctors hear from patients. But there is help, and it is not a heavy drug that leaves you feeling hung-over the next morning—it also isn't late-night television.

First, we must understand the anatomy of normal sleep patterns that, thankfully, most of us enjoy. A researcher by the name of Nathaniel Kleitman observed and reported a phenomenon that occurs during sleep called "rapid eye movement," known as the REM period. As we go to sleep, our body relaxes, and we move into different stages of sleep that identify how deep our sleep is. After about the first ninety minutes or so of sleep, we begin a period where our eyes move rapidly underneath our closed lids. This is the REM period and is the time when we dream. Dreaming is an essential element in good mental health.

While we dream—and absolutely everyone does—our mind is free to deal with our worries and fears by helping us deliberate on possible courses of action to take. Our emotions have a free-for-all, usually in a nonintrusive, nonfearful fashion. When you fail to have enough REM periods (about 20 percent of normal sleep time), sleep deprivation occurs, and you begin to develop uncomfortable symptoms such as irritability, confusion, depression, and general instability.

To make a strong point, sleep deprivation is a common form of torture and has been used on prisoners for "reprogramming" (brainwashing). Many of us who spend restless, sleepless nights can relate. Sleep is absolutely essential to our health and well-being. Most researchers believe that seven to eight hours of sleep is the normal amount most people require, and five hours is the minimum. Remember, it must be uninterrupted sleep to allow for sufficient REM periods.

Causes of Insomnia

Insomnia has a whole host of causes, but these are the most prevalent:

1. *Drug-Dependency Insomnia.* When you take alcohol, barbiturates, or benzodiazapines, your REM period is diminished. When medication is withdrawn to avoid addiction, people go through a difficult time, but gradually eliminating the drugs will eventually restore normal sleep. It isn't just prescription medications that cause problems. Caffeine, alcohol, nicotine, and the endless over-the-counter medications can compromise your ability to get a good night's rest. Many products used by folks to relieve allergy or cold symptoms, not to mention

appetite suppressants and asthma products, contain ingredients that can stimulate you and prevent sleep.
2. *Depression Insomnia.* When someone is depressed, they may experience difficulty falling asleep and staying asleep. Interrupted sleep, especially in the early morning, is common.
3. *Stress Insomnia.* Excessive amounts of stress, worry, and anxiety do not make for adequate rest. An overly demanding lifestyle, not keeping a sleep routine, and poor general health practices are precursors of insomnia. (A more in-depth look at stress is the subject for Chapter 5.)

There is a litany of other origins of insomnia. A good starting place is a visit to your family doctor in order to rule out other possible causes such as sleep apnea, phase-lag syndrome, or any of the eighty-some-odd identified sleep disorders. After a careful medical history and evaluation, your physician may then refer you to a sleep specialist. Sophisticated tests can often ferret out the cause and develop a personalized treatment regime so that you can close those baby blues (or whatever color your eyes may be) and get some well deserved zzz's.

Circadian Rhythm

We all know people who describe themselves as either morning people or night people, and, like most, we are each probably aware of our own natural proclivity regarding when we function most efficiently. This is actually a biological process, not merely a personal whim relative to convenience. Circadian rhythm is the scientific name that describes an individual's sleep and energy cycle. It is an inherent timing mechanism that is associated with brain function, including hormones, amino acids, electrolytes, and neurotransmitters, to name just a few. This powerful collection of biological responses explains in part why birds fly south in the winter and why whales and other mammals, fish, and fowl follow specific migration patterns.

Part of the fascinating functions of your natural circadian rhythm is the impact of body temperature and the ways that hot and cold can be key regulating factors. When I present a lecture to graduate students, I have a little secret I like to use—I turn the air conditioner up to around 72 degrees Fahrenheit. I would like to think that people pay attention and absorb every word I have to say, but the truth is, I know better than that. Obviously, some of my lectures are perhaps more entertaining than others, but by regulating the temperature a few degrees, I am more likely to keep them awake and concentrating on what I'm telling them. When your body temperature is raised, you function more alertly and more efficiently. Typically, your body cycles to higher degrees during the daytime and falls at night, which helps to make you sleep better. I have attended lectures when just the opposite is tried—the lecturer lowers the temperature, and the result is the antithesis of what was desired. People focus on how cold they are and nothing is gained; they then nod off.

When my children were young, I saw patients early during the day and adjusted my schedule accordingly. At home, it was a struggle because I tend to be a night owl. Now that they are grown, I indulge myself and never see my first appointment until 1:00 P.M. It actually works out very well because so many people who work during the day can see me in the afternoon or evening. Unfortunately, not everyone can manipulate their own hours, and, if your career demands are such that you must work evenings or nights, sleep becomes a problem.

Regardless of your own natural rhythms, the group most adversely affected are people who must rotate shift work. Working nights one month and then days the following month and evenings the third is very hard on people. Studies routinely identify a higher degree of work-related accidents, more sick days, absenteeism, and lowered overall performance. Mental health problems dramatically increase as well, and the complaints can be directly correlated with lack of sleep. Many businesses, police and fire departments, and certainly hospitals, which must be staffed twenty-four hours a day, have taken significant steps as a result of these studies to ensure better care and working conditions for their employees. The establishment of a four-day week and twelve-hour shifts has been successful, as well as recognizing the logic of permanent shifts and eliminating rotations.

You can "reset" your natural circadian rhythm, but it takes some effort. Charles P. Pollack, M.D., of New York Hospital–Cornell Medical Center in White Plains, New York, has devised a procedure to get your biology in tune with your life circumstances. He suggests a "sleep progression plan" that puts off sleep over a period of time until you are sleeping correctly. For example, on the first night, rather than going to bed at 2:00 A.M., which, let's say, is your preference, make yourself stay awake until 4:00 A.M. Make certain that you get your usual six to eight hours of sleep, which means you will awake around 11:00 A.M. That night hold off another few hours, repeating the process. It is a gradual correction, but after a week or so, you will have accomplished your target sleep pattern. The next step is the most difficult and the most crucial—you have to stick to it. Sleeping pills only further confuse things, so avoid the temptation. And don't forget to lower the temperature of the room.

Behavioral Helpers

Changes in your lifestyle may be warranted. Using my relaxation tape to teach you how to be peaceful is a great adjunct. I know that I have said this before, but regular exercise and a healthy diet are also essential.

The following are suggestions you can begin using immediately to enhance the quality of your sleep:

- Always try to go to bed at about the same time each night (understand that this is easier said than done) and arise at a scheduled hour.
- Before retiring, begin to wind down, perhaps an hour before.
- Relax by taking a warm bath and do not allow yourself to think about problems.
- The minute you begin to think of something unpleasant say "STOP," and immediately think of something pleasant.
- Some people enjoy listening to music or reading something light just before bed.

Herbs for Your Nerves

◄ Chamomile ►

How about an herb to calm you? Reported in *The Journal of Clinical Pharmacology,* a study was conducted by Dr. Lawrence on patients who were undergoing cardiac catheterization. To say the least, this is a very uncomfortable procedure. According to the research, chamomile tea induced sleep in ten out of the twelve subjects. Chamomile tea is derived from dried flowers of the same name. This lovely flower is a member of the daisy family and is widely used for multiple purposes in Europe, the United States, and Asia.

Chamomile has three properties that make it so popular for treatment:

- An antispasmodic that primarily works on the digestive tract
- An anti-inflammatory agent often used topically on eczema as well as internally
- A mild sedative

Fresh as a daisy is how you may feel after drinking chamomile the night before. According to the *German Commission E Monograph,* pour hot water over approximately 3 grams of *matricaria* flowers. Steep for ten minutes, and then pour through a strainer. This herb also comes in capsule form. You would want to take chamomile one hour prior to bedtime.

There is a precaution with chamomile. Though rare, some people have reported that they developed a rash and shortness of breath after taking this herb. Obviously, you should discontinue using chamomile if such symptoms occur.

◄ Hops ►

Many people know that the hops plant is utilized for both flavor and as a preservative in beer. But it also may explain that "relaxed feeling" you may experience after drinking a beer. From Native Americans to European royalty, hops has been used to induce sleep. Long ago, physicians would suggest stuffing a pillow with hops and placing it under a patient's head. An unidentified oil may be responsible for the sedative effect, and what patients lacked in comfort was made up for in sleep. This leafy, hale plant grows almost anywhere—from Israel to England. The usual dose when given as a fluid extract is 2.0 to 5.8 grams. If you are adventurous and don't mind a lumpy, prickly pillow, get the dried herbs, add a little water and glycerin, and enjoy—if you can—and put an end to your insomnia.

◄ Lady's Slipper ►

Lady's slipper gets its name from the Latin, *Cypripedium parviflorum*. The first part of the name translates as "little shoe," in reference to the slipperlike shape of the flower. The remainder of the name translates as "small flower," in reference to the smaller flower of this variety. Lady's slipper has long been used to cure different ailments. Various Native American tribes used lady's slipper as a nerve medicine. Of late, it has been used to cure insomnia.

Lady's slipper may be confused with valerian root (used to make Valium), but it is milder than valerian. It is used to reduce the effects of anxiety, restlessness, and hysteria. To use lady's slipper, mix .05 to 2.0 grams of the powdered root with two cups of boiling water. Drink one tablespoon at a time throughout the day.

◄ Anemone ►

Anemone use is traced back to the Chinese and Greeks, who used anemone to relieve skin ulcers, inflamed eyes, toothaches, swollen gums, and even for dysentery. Anemone contains anemonin, which causes a depressant effect on the central nervous system. It slows circulation and respiration and has sedative properties. **Caution:** Anemone can slow down respiration so much that *it may result in paralysis and/or death.* To use anemone, take 0.13 to 0.2 gram of the dried powder or 4.6 to 7.8 milliliters over a twenty-four-hour period.

◄ Celery Seeds ►

As convenient as your neighborhood grocery store, celery seeds may offer help when a good night's sleep is needed. They have long been used by herbalists to treat both arthritis and rheumatism. Celery seeds are often combined with willow bark. This common green stalk plant with its willowy leaves can be cooked, grated, or eaten raw, utilizing the entire plant. It contains potassium, chlorides, and sodium, and is believed to help lower blood pressure, quiet spasms in smooth muscles, and reduce flatulence in the intestinal tract.

There are no known side effects when eaten in normal quantities in your diet. Some research suggests that pregnant women should avoid celery because it may cause uterine contractions. Animal studies have found celery seeds to have a soothing property, perhaps due to phthalides.

To use celery seeds for sleep, you can make a tea

using a 5-milliliter tincture, or check out the herbal tea section at a store.

◄ Lavender ►

And of course, don't forget your aromatherapy! British researchers reported in the conservative and extremely prestigious *Lancet* (the British equivalent of the *Journal of the American Medical Association*) that patients who suffered from insomnia were able to sleep through the night when the scent of lavender was present in their bedroom. It seems that this lovely soothing scent is associated with increased alpha waves, which induce relaxation.

Please see Chapter 3 for other herbs beneficial for treating insomnia: Valerian and Passion Flower.

Remember: Never use more than two or three herbs at a time, and *always* check it out with your family doctor first. Herbs can be very helpful if taken correctly and in the proper dosages.

Chapter 5
Stress

The voice of intelligence . . . is drowned out by the roar of fear. It is ignored by the voice of desire. It is contradicted by the voice of shame. It is biased by hate and extinguished by anger. Most of all, it is silenced by ignorance.
—*Karl A. Menninger*

When one person in the family is having difficulties, everyone is affected. Families tend to operate as a "system" with each individual or "part" impacting on the "whole." This is very important to understand and recognize because one person in the family who is under considerable stress can "infect" everybody else. Please let me explain.

A patient of mine who had a highly stressful career (stressful professions include attorney, policeman, teacher, business owner, doctor, parent) always felt under the gun. Because he was a real estate agent, he felt he had very little control over his livelihood, which indeed fluctuated positively or negatively with the local and national economy. My patient was married, had three children, and he and his wife were expecting their fourth child. They had just purchased their new home, and he felt the strain of having to produce a monthly income to maintain their lifestyle. The trickle-down theory was alive and well. He described himself as a grouch around the kids and not always patient with his wife. She began to have some early contractions and was ordered by the doctor to be on bed rest. Unfortunately, this meant her mother had to move in, and three guesses who didn't get along with his mother-in-law!

My patient was stressed, his wife was stressed, and the kids followed suit. We had our work cut out for us!

Stress is not a new concept; the central difference between an earlier era and ours is that we have put a name to it. Dr. Keith Schnert offers one definition of stress: "an imbalance between perceived demand of a stressful event, and the perceived response capabilities of the individual, which results in difficulties in coping, and begins the degenerative compromise of the immune system, resulting in illness."

You would possibly agree that stress in and of itself does not always lead to illness. Good stress, I believe, may be part and parcel of—or even actually synonymous with—motivation. So, if we look at the "doers" in our society, we may be looking at people who make stress work to their advantage.

The more complex your lifestyle, the more juggling you are asked to do. I see a lot of women in my practice who are at their breaking point because they place upon themselves Herculean demands that three people would be hard-pressed to accomplish.

Just like my patient's wife, they may be concerned about financial support (food and shelter), marital problems, and the care of children. The companion emotions are fear, guilt, and feeling overwhelmed. The men who come to see me often have a parallel history, but with some variations. They tend to focus more on their career demands, business issues, employer–employee conflicts, frustrations, and concerns for the future. Sometimes these men are the single breadwinners. In our society we rear women to be caregivers and men "to fix things." When a man is confronted with situations he can't "fix"—the economy, a sick child, a wife's needs—he often becomes angry, frustrated, and then withdraws into himself. I think we just described my patient—with some modifications!

Causes of Stress

Despite our fantasies, no one can live without stress.

It is the "motivation" that underpins all achievement, and when you manage it properly, you can use it to assist the healing process and prevent disease.

I want to emphasize that stress is the result of subtle or not-so-subtle micro and macro stressors. Examples of micro stressors may be low-volume but constant background noise, constant little irritations, stagnant or unhappy relationships, or ongoing, never resolved problems at your place of employment. Micro stressors tend to keep things stirred up but are not personally earthshaking in nature. They include worry, tension, and annoyances. Macro stressors, on the other hand, stand up and grab your attention, and they include devastating events such as death, divorce, being fired, or situations such as poverty, bankruptcy, an impossible-to-please boss, or traumas such as illness, drug abuse, moving, or the end of a romance.

Think about the micro and macro stressors in your life. List three in each of the following categories:

Home and Family
1. _____
2. _____
3. _____

Professional or Job Related
1. _____
2. _____
3. _____

Personal and Relationships
1. _____
2. _____
3. _____

The most common reason people feel stressed is because they feel they have no control. The situation is either out of hand, or they feel trapped and without any choice. You always have a choice. Admittedly, the choices may not appear to be good ones, but you do have a choice. Once you begin saying that message to yourself, you will start feeling in control. For instance, take the image you chose when I asked you in the preceding example to imagine a stressor from your job, and ask yourself this question:

What can I do to change the situation?

If you cannot come up with a change, then you have two rational choices:

1. You must adapt to and accept the situation.
   OR
2. You must find another job.

I encourage people to take risks, but I ask them to do so thoughtfully. If you hate your job and it causes you stress, please find another one! Life is too short to be stressed out and unhappy. If you are involved in a miserable relationship, again, do something different—accept things as they are or get out! From feeling trapped or feeling like a victim springs anger and turmoil—so take control! Find some peace and happiness. You deserve to be treated with kindness and respect. Don't settle for anything less. **Bad jobs and/or bad relationships = poor self-image**. Again, remember that you always have two choices:

1. You must adapt to and accept the situation.
   OR
2. You can get out.

Managing our stressors is paramount to good mental health. It is important to be able to distinguish stress from depression. I will help you differentiate the two in this chapter, briefly. Depression will be covered more fully in another chapter.

When I contrast the symptoms of stress and depression, I usually add psychological correlates to disease. These correlates are character traits or issues that are really symptoms in disguise. They are some of the reasons why people get sick.

I often think these differences become confused in our label-happy society. Some of the symptoms of depression seem to overlap stress symptoms. Stress in many ways can set the stage for a serious depression, and depression often is the by-product of stress—and so is burnout. There are several types of depression, including one that seems to have a genetic or inherited component, but there is no doubt in my mind that stress can also trigger a depressive episode. Stress often acts as a precursor to depression. Stress symptoms are warnings from our body signaling us to change course or slow down. Such messages should be heeded.

Remember, stress is the imbalance between perceived demands of a stressful event and the perceived response capabilities of the individual. Whether this imbalance is great or small results in differences in coping with the stress. If the imbalance is great, then the inability to cope begins the degeneration and compromise of the immune system, resulting in illness.

Psychological

Correlates to Disease

unresolved family-of-origin

stoicism

self-destruction

feelings of loss

compliance

self-sacrificing

denial of anger

inability to show emotions

caretaker

Symptoms of Stress

headaches

anxiety, nervousness

- feeling angry or hostile
- muscle tension
- low performance
- irritability
- forgetfulness
- feeling overloaded
- gastrointestinal problems

Symptoms of Depression

- lack of concentration
- low feelings of self-worth
- "what is the use" attitude
- thoughts of suicide
- weight loss or gain
- difficulty sleeping
- feeling angry
- feeling overwhelmed
- exhaustion

Our perception can act as a de-stressing mechanism. If we revisit Dr. Schnert's definition, we can see that he talks about "perception" as a tool to de-stress ourselves. Perception is the way we, as individuals, "see" and "interpret" an event. Because everyone is different and comes from different backgrounds, we do not always "perceive" or "see" things the same. We know that one person's description of an event is 180 degrees different from that of two or three others. It is akin to the old "rumor game" where eight to twenty people sitting in a circle begin with a brief story that is whispered to each person by the previous person and, at the end, the last person tells the story. The simple story at the beginning no longer resembles in any way the final "rumor"! Are people lying? No, they are perceiving, based on their own value systems, life experiences, family backgrounds, religions, and socioeconomic status.

Ask any police officer who arrives at the scene of an accident and begins to interview witnesses, and he or she will verify perception in action. The various accounts of the accident are explained by this concept.

Let's look at my patient and see how changing your perception can de-stress you. By looking at the event in a different fashion, you can reduce your feelings of angst. Because his wife is not doing well and has to stay in bed (Mom is not that much help), he is in charge and must assume some of her responsibilities, as well as his normal duties. What if we take this same situation or "event" and change his perception:

Same Event, Different Perceptions

Stressing

I feel totally overwhelmed.

I am unsure of my ability to deal with this crisis.

It is just too much—so what's the use?

Boy, does my head hurt.

I feel like I am going to explode.

De-stressing

This situation is a big challenge—but I have dealt with worse so I am up for it.

I've always managed in the past, so I can conquer this one as well.

I feel energized and enthusiastic!

My patient is now in a problem-solving mode, enlisting help from friends and neighbors, which frees up time for him to work more. This, in turn, has a calming effect on his wife, and with the added help, her mother can go home (or just help out occasionally)!

Behavioral Helpers

As you just saw, the difference between those people who control stress and those people whom stress controls is often defined by our perceptions. Before I give you herbal suggestions, there are some behavioral helpers to consider. I call them "light promoters," and they act as stress filters. As you will see, they clearly outline lifestyle changes as well as psychological changes.

One of the main principles in stress management is to maintain a strong foundation by practicing good health and fitness. This certainly includes eating correctly and exercising regularly. Proper rest is important as well.

Becoming more aware of yourself and others will help you identify early signs of stress. What kind of demands are on you and how are you handling them? Can you anticipate stressful events and begin early coping strategies?

It is also very important to take responsibility for your actions—this helps you feel more in control and empowered. Remember that blame and excuses in the long run can cause anger and pain and lead to "victim" feelings.

Look for inner strength through relaxation techniques, quiet time, or meditation. Those are three wonderful and effective ways to reduce stress. Be kind to yourself and maintain patience toward your imperfections and adversity. Focus on how far you have come!

Another helpful de-stressor is through the maintenance of a strong support system, which may consist of your family and/or friends. Being able to express fear, anger, and frustration reduces emotional pressures and bonds you with others. A support system can provide warmth and encouragement and can give you other people's insights on stress management. Along these same lines, these family members or friends can assist you in problem solving and decision-making.

The creation of a personal stability zone can go a long way toward de-stressing. Examples of such a zone might include a special chair, listening to or performing music, or even wearing an article of clothing such as an old bathrobe.

One of the best de-stressors often suggested and

supported by research is a pet. There has been much research in an area called psychoneuroimmunology, which is an extremely large word to describe the things we have just discussed. One of the strongest recommendations that comes out of this research is evidence of the benefits provided by pets. Many nursing homes are using pet therapy to help patients cope with anxiety and loneliness. A dog, cat, fish, bunny, or the like is a wonderful addition to any stress/de-stress program.

Albert Einstein said that "imagination is more important than knowledge." As you go through the rest of your life, reflect upon this message. Keep in your mind the idea that what you believe is exactly what you can achieve and that your imagination along with your beliefs and experiences helps you create a new beginning or more of the old stuff that does not serve you in a loving way. Every day is an opportunity to embrace and honor the best parts of yourself and love the imperfections as well. This is the cornerstone of stress management.

There are some things we must accept as part of life. One is that the past is just that—gone and unchangeable. Another is that no matter how hard we try, like the past, we cannot change others. Attempting to do so leaves you upset, exhausted, and stressed out.

But what is exciting and absolutely changeable is the way you view your past and how you view those important people in your life. To state this concept more plainly—*you* can change *you!* You have the power to make yourself happy. Understand that life is perhaps only a small portion of what happens to you, but what happens to you is a large portion of how you react to it. Choose your reactions carefully.

Herbs for Your Nerves

◄ Eleuthero ►

A 2,000-year-old herb called eleuthero, or siberian ginseng, is the root of choice for stress. It comes to us from Russia with love and is used by their cosmonauts and athletes for a variety of reasons, among which are to increase mental and physical performance, confront chronic fatigue, and boost the immune system.

Eleuthero is a rather unattractive, skinny, prickly little shrub, but what it lacks in beauty it more than makes up for in stress relief. It helps to heal the body, which helps to heal the mind.

Solid extracts of the standardized eleutherosides B and E with a dose of 300 to 400 milligrams daily for six to eight weeks are recommended. Skip one or two weeks and then begin the regimen again.

◄ Kava Kava ►

Kava kava may also be a consideration for stress as it tends to induce a state of relaxation but does not interfere with memory! The plant can be found growing on the Pacific Islands and enjoys a rather colorful history.

It seems that Samoan, Fiji, and other Polynesian chieftains sometimes used kava kava during special ceremonial rites. Perhaps overused is a better description. At a safe dose you relax, but overdosing may cause hallucinations. Some ceremonies were more special than others.

The usual dose of standardized extract containing 70 percent kava lactones is 100 milligrams taken two or three times a day. It may take up to two months to work, so you need to be patient. Once you have achieved a comfortable level, you may then reduce the dose. Used as directed, it is safe, but high doses can cause dizziness or a rash. Do not take kava kava if you are pregnant or nursing, using alcohol, or if you are taking prescribed antidepressants or tranquilizers.

◄ Valerian ►

A third herb you might use to reduce stress symptoms is valerian, which we discussed in Chapter 3, "Anxiety." You may take eleuthero and valerian together, initially, if you wish. The recommended dosage for valerian is 300 to 500 milligrams taken an hour before bedtime.

◄ Lemon Grass ►

Lemon grass is a popular plant that many cultures have used in their traditional medicine. In Brazil, it has long been used as a sedative. In other parts of South America, it has also been used to treat fevers and as an antispasmodic. In India, it is commonly used as an antirheumatic and antiseptic.

In Cuba, lemon grass is an integral part of traditional medicine. The National Center for Scientific Research in Havana tested lemon grass on rats. In their studies, lemon grass produced an immediate drop in blood pressure that endured for up to thirty-five minutes. However, some tests on lemon grass (in tea form) show that it does not produce any noticeable results.

Lemon grass in oil form is used in aromatherapy and produces calming effects. It is widely used as a sedative. Lemon grass produces no known toxic effects on humans.

◄ Vitamin O ►

And have you heard about the new kid on the block—vitamin O? With the advent of hyperbaric oxygen chambers (more recently made famous by Michael Jackson) to wage war on such diseases and conditions as the bends and gangrene, O_2 is now the rage. A not so uncommon sight in Japan, O_2 bars are popping up in America. Cities like New York and Chicago have regular patrons.

Pollution levels in many of the world's cities are so high that the oxygen content is dangerously low. Symptoms that are consistent with oxygen depletion include weakness, muscular aches, fatigue, respiratory distress, memory loss, and irrational behavior. Alone or in combination, these complaints seem vague and difficult to understand. When the human body is oxygen-deficient, normal oxidation of substances that are vital to our health is compromised. Our immune system comes under attack and is profoundly stressed.

Apart from breathing oxygen, several "supplements" have been developed. Stabilized oxygen was used by NASA to help sustain astronauts and to maximize their safety. Check with your health food store for further references.

◄ Geranium ►

When you wish to decrease stress in your life, a good aromatherapy suggestion is the scent of geranium. This essential oil can be used alone or in conjunction with sweet marjoram or ylang-ylang.

Remember: Never use more than two or three herbs at a time and *always* check it out with your family doctor first.

Chapter 6
Depression

*And nothing to look backward
to with pride.
And nothing to look forward
to with hope.*

—Robert Frost,
"The Death of the Hired Hand," 1924

Sometimes things have a way of building. You may begin by having some symptoms consistent with anxiety, but which progress into insomnia. When you are anxious and losing sleep, you are bound to feel stress. Then compounding these symptoms, depression rears its ugly head. The result is a downward spiral whose hallmarks are sadness and feeling out of control. The trick here is to develop some awareness before you head for the bottom.

Depression can be defined as "anger turned inward." Nice people often become depressed because they lack the facility to express their emotions. Saying "no" to people and re-establishing limits are foreign ideas. They feel used and taken advantage of but suppress these feelings with multiple layers of denial. All of this "stuffing" can lead to depression.

Depression is often associated with loss. Sometimes the loss is very obvious and may be related to being fired, the breakup of a relationship, or even a move. But other times the loss may be elusive or nebulous—something you can't put your finger on—for example, unresolved family-of-origin issues, abuse, or low self-esteem.

Of all the problems that I see in my practice, depression is probably number one in frequency. More often than not, it is accompanied by a history of physical, emotional, or sexual abuse and/or low self-esteem. Our self-esteem is the sum total of our experiences and genetic makeup. Which of these is the most influential is still being argued.

Patients will come to me complaining of vague symptoms such as feelings of emptiness, procrastination, or self-depreciative thoughts, which they are quick to verbalize. Physical symptoms such as headaches or muscular pain often accompany the more typical signs.

It has been estimated that one out of ten people in our society suffers from depression. Based on my professional experience, I believe this is a very conservative statistic. Many people walk around feeling depressed, but do not recognize it as such, so it goes unreported and, worse, untreated.

Scientifically, we refer to the collective types of depression as Affective Disorders, and classify them as either primary depression (feeling depressed) or secondary depression (feeling depressed but you also have another psychiatric disorder that may have triggered the depression).

Primary depression can be either unipolar (again, just depressed) or bipolar, which refers to depressed periods alternating with periods of elation or mania. These classifications break down further, but for our purposes we will limit our discussion to primary depression.

While I concur that herbs can help with the overall well-being of someone who suffers from manic depression, this is a disorder that clearly requires medication. The same is true for someone who is severely depressed, but for mild or moderate depression, herbs may be very helpful.

A depressed mood may be described as "feeling the blues." Patients report a sense of gloominess, sadness, and an inability to experience the normal pleasures of life. It is interesting to take another look at the psychological correlates (traits) to depression with the symptoms manifested by the patient. The psychological correlates in the table are interchangeable with the symptoms listed. Each correlate may be expressed by a variety of symptoms.

Psychological Correlates

1. Unresolved conflict associated with family-of-origin issues, careers, or relationships; past or present abuse including physical, psychological, or sexual abuse
2. Stoicism or inability to express feelings and thoughts to others
3. Self-destruction, self-sabotage, poor physical health maintenance
4. Sense of loss, grief
5. Compliance, possibly with accompanying thoughts of resentment
6. Self-sacrificing; martyr; caretaker
7. Denied or suppressed anger
8. Inability to show emotion; tendency to isolate oneself

Symptoms of Depression

1. Lack of concentration or preoccupation with problems
2. Low feelings of self-worth with a false bravado; anxiety, poor self-esteem, unrealistic expectations, poor performance
3. "What's the use" attitude; "Is this all there is?"
4. Self-deprecatory thoughts, intrusive thoughts, or obsessing

5. Weight loss or weight gain; gastrointestinal complaints
6. Sleep disturbance: too much, too little, or interrupted. Muscle tensions, headaches
7. Violent outbursts of rage
8. Feeling overwhelmed, forgetful, irritable, exhausted

These symptoms can be common to even a mild depression, but they differ in terms of intensity and duration. It is the *extreme* that differentiates a mild to moderate depression from a major depression. Therefore, if we look at our table, we would have to add an additional heading:

Major Depression
- Inability to concentrate
- Demeaning and accusatory thoughts
- Substance abuse; running away
- Thoughts of suicide
- Greater or lesser ten-pound fluctuation in weight
- Insomnia or excessive sleeping; anxiety
- Rage and agitation
- Inability to cope
- Inability to function

Obviously, these symptoms require immediate intervention and professional help, especially if someone is suicidal. Please do not waste time—take swift action. But if you find yourself with just a mild to moderate depression, there are many options you might try.

Those of us who have been in medical or mental health practice for even a few years are quick to recognize the connection between the mind and the body. This link is vital because how the two interrelate can make us sick or well, succeed or fail. Modern medicine with all of its heralded and well-deserved praise cannot "make" a person well who does not wish to be well. We have at our disposal a whole array of techniques, medications, and procedures to carefully diagnose and treat even the most profound physical or mental illness, but with all of these assets we can do little if the patient believes in or desires a negative outcome.

How does someone become depressed? The etiology or genesis of depression has more than one cause, and the following is a brief summary.

Genetics

There seems to be a genetic link to depression that is supported by studies but is not completely understood. We know depression runs in families, but the gene has not been identified. Researchers also have found increased evidence regarding the brain's biochemistry and its relation to depression. Our neurotransmitters—in particular norepinephrine and serotonin—affect our moods. We know this because when antidepressants are given, the chemical change brings relief. What is interesting about genetics is that not all genes are expressed and not every member of the family inherits the bad ones. What most neurobiologists do agree upon is that we are about 75 to 80 percent the result of our biology and only 20 to 25 percent our environment. But that 20 to 25 percent can be critical.

Psychodynamics

The importance of "the hand that rocks the cradle" cannot be dismissed. Parents are our first teachers, and they model the behaviors, beliefs, and attitudes that impact us all of our lives. They teach us how to parent, conduct relationships, and strongly influence career paths, happiness, and success. From them our self-image emerges, values are developed, and coping strategies are learned. How we get along with others and feel about ourselves often can be traced to childhood.

The connection of abuse with depression has been well documented. A disturbing reflection of this fact is recognition of the number of patients suffering from multiple personality disorders as the result of sexual abuse in childhood. Abuse does not need to be sexual, however, to cause damage. Verbal abuse as well as physical abuse, sexual abuse, and neglect are all lethal. Children who are told how disappointed their parents are with them, that they are dumb, stupid, and useless, give up and quite often fulfill their parents' damaging predictions. They adopt their parents' self-fulfilling prophecy.

These children grow into angry adults, often depressed, not understanding why life just does not seem to bring any pleasure or peace of mind. They often drop in and out of marriages, careers, and friendships, never able to keep things together, longing for the intimacy that eludes them. Such is the legacy of verbal abuse. As with sexual and verbal abuse, physical abuse destroys the child's sense of trust and incapacitates the sense of self, leaving deep and pervasive scars in the psyche.

Adults who grow up in homes where alcohol and drugs were used and misused can repeat the pattern or can suffer depression, with the root cause as substance abuse. Violence is also a learned behavior. Thankfully, most adults do come from better beginnings, and of those who did not, their legacy is not etched in stone. Many become exemplary spouses, parents, and citizens, contributing greatly to society.

Cognitive theory suggests that people who view the world with negativity are more prone to depression. This may be the result of learned behavior from parents whose ideas and actions are permeated with negative thinking. My belief is that depressed people have a genetic predisposition, and that unresolved childhood conflicts may trigger a biochemical imbalance that results in depression. Further, situations may occur that have nothing to do with genetics, psychodynamics, or cognitive theory. Life just happens!

There are doctors in both fields of medicine and psychology who hold that people create their own illness, unhappiness, and failures, that we somehow allow ourselves to become sick. Perhaps by thinking certain thoughts and holding certain beliefs one may somehow invoke sickness into life, physically or emotionally, not to mention failure and pain. Obviously, there are myriad reasons people become depressed, and not all are self-inflicted. The world is like a mirror, and our seeing pain, dishonor, hatred, and prejudice often may be simply a reflection of what is going on inside of us. The cures come as we change our minds and hearts.

Anger

Anger is often associated with depression, and I am including it in this discussion because I believe it possesses many biological/genetic/brain-damage/disease traits that somehow explain depression. With anger the origin is not always clear. For example, a closed head injury can be the cause of anger and depression. However, my discussion will be looking at anger in general and not in the sense of injury or a physical or medical problem.

Anger is a basic emotion, but one that we don't like to discuss. Yet this very lack of discussion generates and escalates more anger. Anger is a learned response, usually from our parents. The purpose of anger is to neutralize, protect, or avoid anxiety, which rears its ugly head whenever we feel an interpersonal threat. When a little kid is frustrated, usually as a result of unsuccessfully challenging the authority of Mom or Dad, he or she notices this amazing rage of anger that is generated by the parent. So the child then makes the intuitive connection between the uncomfortable and powerless anxiety feelings that he or she has felt and expressed by trying to manipulate parents through tears, and the extreme power gained by converting those feelings into anger. Anger is distinctly more powerful than anxiety. The degree and method to which a child uses this "power" can be helpful or hurtful, and the stakes increase as he or she becomes an adult.

The price some people pay for anger is feeling victimized by forces beyond their control such as might occur in employee/employer problems, finances, and relationships. They feel that advantages and luck are for *other* people and that they themselves are powerless and weak. Often they are not even aware of these feelings, especially if they come from a family where anger and conflict were not allowed or discussed. Even if they do temporarily overcome their feelings of intimidation and speak up, they are consumed with guilt for having done so and then give up on life. For others, they fear that if they let out their anger, they might hurt someone or that if they really let out their anger fully, they could go crazy. The real truth is that unexpressed anger can lead to depression, suicide, a major illness, or a violent outburst of rage—the very same outcomes people are attempting to avoid by bottling up their anger to begin with.

Anger is an emotion that generates physiological changes and produces feelings that often impact on your self-image and perception of life events. Anger can serve several behavioral functions. For example, anger may announce to others by various means of expression how you are feeling or what your position on a specific issue may be. It may be a warning that signals an action. Anger can be an effective but damaging way to control or influence others. Anger is a necessary emotion that helps us to survive in a sometimes difficult life. It is an emotion, and, like any other emotion, it is okay to feel it. Anger can help us find the strength necessary to stop feeling helpless and to feel empowered rather than victimized. It most assuredly does not have to culminate in violence.

Anger produces a wide range of physiological changes—many of which can actually be measured by chemical assays, EEGs, blood tests, and computers. Some typical responses include:

- Changes in muscle tension
- Vascular changes, flushing or paling
- Sweating
- Clenching of fists or teeth
- Dry mouth
- Difficulty thinking
- Change in voice
- Fright
- Aggression

One very provocative finding by researchers investigating anger was that while some people felt physically ill by anger, others reported a feeling of exhilaration. This tends to lend credibility to those of us who see anger, when appropriately channeled, as a great motivator. People tend to be motivated either away (avoidance) from pain or toward (approach) pleasure. The approachers may find their situation so terrible and become so angry that they will use that anger as fuel to accomplish greatness. Some common comments you may hear are, "Well, I'll show you," "I am going to make them eat those words," or "I don't care what Dad said, I will be successful."

Researchers have also tried to identify and categorize things that make people angry. One category was "stupid inanimate objects"—things that don't work, like a pen out of ink, vending machines that take your money, and so forth. A second category was "special aversions" such as little habits or quirks people have that are annoying. But the third category, "injustice to others," was the one most people identified as the most anger-arousing. Insults, cheating, abuse, and being condescending were high on the list.

Some people, for seemingly no reason at all, can erupt spontaneously into a rage, creating verbal and physical violence. A tumultuous storm in the brain produces just such expressed rage and has now been identified as a seizure. Furthermore, neurological deficits and outbursts of rage may be the result of child abuse.

Allergies, especially to certain foods, have reportedly produced rage, though this is very rare. Disease or damage associated with the temporal lobe in the brain, Alzheimer's disease, Huntington's chorea, tumors, and head injuries are causes that produce rage attacks. Further, genetic and other organic defects, birth injuries, and infantile convulsions are frequently reported as possible causes for the rage suffered by some people.

Dorothy O. Lewis studied juvenile delinquents imprisoned for violence and found that physical trauma corresponds directly to increasingly violent behavior. Again, angry, abusive parents not only "show" children how to "act" and "respond," but in the course of the abuse, may inflict neurological injuries that cause violence. It must be stated here, however, that only about one-third of physically or sexually abused people continue the same pattern with their children. Most, through education and personal strength, have learned more appropriate methods to deal with anger and go out of their way to stop the cycle.

Anger then tends to be associated with incidents about which you are aware (for example, you see someone flip you off while you are driving) and with ones you are not (for example, something triggers a suppressed feeling, or, less often, there is a biological problem). A more common cause of anger has to do with how we perceive an incident—our own interpretation of an event. In a nutshell, anger can be either self-generated or a reaction to environmental demands, and the sources can be physiological, emotional, cognitive, or behavioral. While you cannot control feeling angry, you can control how you act upon it.

Seasonal Affective Disorder (SAD)

Long, cold, dark winters have been linked to a form of depression known as Seasonal Affective Disorder (SAD). The essential feature of this condition is the onset or remission of a major depressive episode, usually during the winter or dark months. The symptoms arrive in late fall and gradually disappear with the light of spring days. Sufferers complain of lack of energy, overeating that results in weight gain, an excessive need to sleep, and a craving for carbohydrates.

SAD is seen more frequently in northern climates and tends to be related to age and gender, affecting a greater number of younger persons and females. Irritable, feeling sad and bored, people with SAD isolate themselves, hibernating like bears.

The cause of this disorder may be the function or lack thereof of the pineal gland, a very small organ located near the center of the brain. The pineal gland releases a hormone called melatonin, which impacts your energy level. Light inhibits the production of melatonin, and, as the lights dim, more melatonin is released, which lowers your energy and makes you feel tired. As an example, if you are living in Alaska and suffer from this disorder, four hours of daylight that is rather dim (a common situation for several months each year) is going to be a problem.

There are several things a SAD patient can try, some very practical and some not so practical. The first suggestion falls under that last category—move to a sunnier climate.

A better option, if moving is not possible, is "light therapy." Patients are instructed to look into special bright lights with 2,500 LUX intensity, which are similar to the ultraviolet light rays from the sun, for periods of three to four hours, twice a day. Regular light bulbs are not as effective. Bulbs that are therapeutic must be strong, bright white lights. Within a few days, people show improvement, but the treatment must be ongoing during the weeks or months of darkness, which may be a bit impractical and time consuming.

Behavioral Helpers

Become more analytical and keep an anger diary. For the next few weeks, write about your anger incidents and answer the following four questions:

1. What is going on that makes me angry?
2. What is the core issue here for me?
3. What are my responsibilities?
4. How can I change this situation and achieve parity and peace?

Specific behavioral help for anger:

1. Carefully consider what is involved in the matter before you turn it into open conflict.
2. Confront the right person in a private place at a convenient time and limit the conflict to the here and now. Do not bring up old issues for ammunition.
3. Discuss only one issue at a time and use the "hard on the issue, soft on the person" approach. Plan and organize your thoughts prior to the confrontation.
4. Always try to use "I" statements and supportive communication. "You" messages are a statement of condemnation; using "I" conveys a feeling.
5. Avoid global generalizations such as "always," "never," "everybody," "all of the time."
6. Confront the behavior, not the attitudes. Do not launch a general attack on the other's personality—no character attacks.
7. No mind reading; no counterattacks. Accept the other's statement as his or her perception. No hitting below the belt.
8. Take responsibility for your actions and feelings. Try to analyze your own participation in the problem, not the other party's participation.
9. Understand that your perception could be wrong.

10. State the problem in behavioral terms, such as "When _____ happens, I feel _____ because _____."
11. Use "active listening" techniques.
12. Make sure that your emotions are proportionate to the crime.
13. Be emotionally supportive. Do not be concerned with winning or losing. What is important is that the problem is solved.

Finding yourself in the midst of a mild or moderate depression is challenging but not hopeless. The rub in this situation is that when you most need to rally your inner resources, you are the least able. To get you going, you need to find someone you trust to talk things out. We call such friends and family a *support system.* If you are new to an area and do not have a support system in place, call the local psychiatric hospital and get a list of support groups. These groups are usually informal and free.

I use bibliotherapy (the new buzz word for an old technique) to assist patients with getting to the core issues with which they must deal. Keeping a journal (in a private place) of your thoughts and feelings on a daily basis helps to put things in perspective and causes a natural emergence of helpful information to come about. Patients tell me all the time how amazed they are at what bubbles up from their unconscious. This intrapsychic material can be examined, encouraging introspection.

Another aspect of bibliotherapy is reading. There are a plethora of fine self-help and inspirational books that can lead to new insights and foster hope. Self-help books may help solve past and present puzzles and may offer numerous resources for relief. These books do not take the place of actual psychotherapy and should be used cautiously. Just because it is in print doesn't make it correct. Keep an open mind.

Feelings of being boxed in with no place to go or of being trapped are often companions to depression. The situation is such that you feel you have no choices, a very depressing thought indeed. But the truth is, we always have choices. Admittedly, sometimes we are faced with choosing between uncomfortable choices—but, nonetheless, they are choices. Making a decision can be very liberating, so here is a good method to help you choose:

How to Make a Decision

Step 1: Identify and write down the issue you must deal with.

Step 2: List the choices you can make and say out loud, "These are my choices."

Step 3: Assess the positives and negatives of your choices. A "pro and con" list clarifies the options.

Step 4: Make a choice and say out loud, "I choose _____." Conscious awareness reminds you who has made the decision. It implies ownership.

Step 5: Say, "I made this choice because _____." Understand consciously why you made this choice.

In this one process you have regained control, garnered information, selected a plan of action, and reduced your feelings of overload. Quite an accomplishment!

Overcoming self-defeating behaviors, or self-sabotage, is another way to work your way through depression. Self-sabotage comes in two forms—physical and emotional. The characteristics of physical self-sabotage include a variety of addictive behaviors such as overeating, substance abuse, or inappropriate amounts of sleep and no exercise.

The flip side is emotional sabotage. Such behaviors as procrastination, anger, tardiness, and lack of motivation are hallmarks of the problem.

One of the most painful but necessary aspects to overcome self-defeating behavior is to become introspective and identify abhorrent patterns. Tracing the genesis of your problems is the first step. Ask yourself how you learned to procrastinate or who taught you how to deal with anger. Chances are you will discover that these defenses originated in childhood and have become your way of avoiding success. If you look back carefully, you will notice that these behaviors never served your parents or mentor any better than they are serving you.

We never do anything without some sort of

"payoff." Unfortunately our payoffs are not always positive. Remember that self-sabotage is a defense—it keeps you from achieving your goals and "protects" you from success. So more questions need to be asked: What am I afraid of and what am I getting out of the sabotage—continued failure and disappointment?

Some folks fear success, others failure, but acknowledging those fears and doing it anyway is essential. One way to overcome self-sabotage is to remember a time when you felt successful, when you accomplished something in spite of yourself. Really feel how good and exhilarating it was, how proud you were of yourself and the confidences that accompanied that feeling.

The next time you begin to slip into a sabotaging behavior, immediately force yourself to feel what you felt when you were successful and act "as if" you have succeeded again. Your subconscious cannot tell the difference between what is real and what is not. So, if you act "as if . . . " you will be on your way to overcoming the negative behavior and replacing it with a positive one.

Herbs for Your Nerves

◄ St. Johnswort ►

Perhaps one of the most exciting succors for mild to moderate depression is a very old herb that is causing a new sensation. St. Johnswort announces its inner beauty with bright yellow blossoms. Dating back to Hippocrates, the plant served a variety of uses from snakebites to kidney problems. It grows wild in the United States in sunny areas.

This little plant has two very unique properties. It is an antidepressant as well as an antiviral agent and is currently being evaluated for its efficacy with AIDS and Herpes Type I and II.

St. Johnswort inhibits monamine oxidase, which ultimately increases norepinephrine and brings about relief from depression. The recommended dosage of St. Johnswort is 900 milligrams daily, divided into three doses. But you need to read the label. An essential active ingredient in the extract is hypericin, which may vary in strength depending on the brand you buy. You want the St. Johnswort extract to contain 0.3% of hypericin.

When using St. Johnswort, you should limit your exposure to the sun or ultraviolet rays because it may cause skin irritation. There are some dietary considerations as well. Avoid smoked or pickled food and alcohol. If you are currently being treated with another antidepressant, stick to that one and do not take St. Johnswort along with it.

Please consider my warnings concerning depression. It can be a life-threatening disease and requires medical treatment in its advanced form. St. Johnswort can certainly help, but is not a substitute for medical attention if your depression is moderately severe to severe. For information on accompanying anxiety or insomnia, see Chapters 3 and 4.

◄ SAM-e ►

SAM-e, short for *S-Adenosylmethionine,* is an over-the-counter dietary supplement said to ease the devastating effects of depression. SAM-e is *not* an herb; it is a natural-forming compound found in all living cells. In humans, SAM-e is found in the brain as part of the molecular makeup.

Normal brain activity includes chemical messengers passing between cells. SAM-e may positively impact the mood-altering boosters—serotonin and dopamine. SAM-e has been shown, in some studies, to be more effective in the treating of depression than current antidepressants.

In one study, seventeen severely depressed patients were split into two groups. The first was given SAM-e in 1,600-milligram daily doses, and the second was given desipramine, another antidepressant. After the four-week treatment, patients using SAM-e had a higher response rate (62 percent) than those using desipramine (50 percent).

To use SAM-e, take two tablets (400 milligrams) daily as a dietary supplement or as directed by a physician. **Caution:** Studies suggest SAM-e may trigger episodes in people who suffer from bipolar disorder. Other side effects include a mild upset stomach.

Sandalwood

In eastern parts of the world, sandalwood has been used for centuries. It was mentioned in Sanskrit and Chinese manuscripts. Its oil was used in religious ceremonies and temples were carved from its wood. Ancient Egyptians imported the wood and used it for medicinal purposes, embalming practices, and religious worship. Sandalwood is a tree native only to forests in parts of Indonesia.

Today, all forms of sandalwood exports are banned by the Indian government. Even so, it is being harvested and exported illegally. Known to many as "Liquid Gold," sandalwood oil, once distilled, is matured for six months.

For more than 4,000 years, sandalwood incense has been used for its calming effects in meditation and yoga. It soothes the mind, enhances mental capability, and regenerates the skin. Perhaps due to these relaxing and calming effects, sandalwood eases the effects of depression.

To use sandalwood, use five to twenty drops of the oil as incense. **Precaution**: While sandalwood is nontoxic and a nonirritant, always consult a physician about serious depression disorders and their treatment.

Jasmine

When someone is depressed, they often have great difficulty getting out of bed and following a normal day's schedule. Depression also makes it difficult to concentrate. If you are not dealing with anxiety, the smell of jasmine may be just what you need. Jasmine used as aromatherapy tends to stimulate the mind and, in general, increases cognitive functioning.

Remember: Never use more than two or three herbs at a time and always check it out with your family doctor first.

Chapter 7
Fatigue

The number of those who undergo the fatigue of judging for themselves is very small indeed.
 —Richard Brinsley Sheridan, The Critic

So many people seem to go through life never feeling energetic, always feeling tired or even exhausted. Ten years ago otherwise seemingly healthy people demonstrated a cluster of symptoms that became labeled as the "Yuppie Virus." Through blood testing, some showed an elevation in their tests to the Epstein-Barr virus. It is estimated that by the time we reach thirty years old, most all of us carry this "bug," but how it is activated is arguable. Not all members of the medical community agree that Chronic Fatigue Syndrome (CFS) is a legitimate disorder, and, sadly, some patients are told that it is all in their head and that, basically, they need to get a grip. This can be a devastating blow to someone who is already down.

Perhaps part of the problem can be assigned to the fact that there are no magic cures—there are no specific medications that can make things all better. Most patients come to their physician with a litany of complaints, some of which may be depression and anxiety. At first glance, it may be decided that this is a psychological problem, and so the patient often is referred to a mental health practitioner. It is difficult enough to be sick, but it is a double whammy when you are dismissed as being a hypochondriac.

To add fodder to the problem is the truth that you probably are depressed. If you suddenly can barely stay awake and are unable to accomplish your job and everyday tasks, of course you are sad and down. But there is hope.

The following symptoms are often associated with Chronic Fatigue Syndrome or Epstein-Barr virus:

- Debilitating fatigue
- Sore throat
- Muscle aches and pain

- Joint pain
- Migraines
- Depression
- Swollen lymph nodes

A study published in the January 1985 issue of the *Annals of Internal Medicine* outlined some fifteen symptoms and noted a "silent epidemic." Patients often minimized their symptoms as did their family members. They were reticent to seek medical attention because their complaints were so vague. Remember that there are different intensities to this syndrome, so some folks just suffered and got on as best they could. Attitudes regarding this syndrome have definitely improved since that time, however, so if these symptoms describe you, please seek help. And if your physician is less than receptive, find one who cares.

Chronic fatigue should not be ignored. It takes a toll on your immune system (the very mechanism that fights off major illnesses) and has been associated with some forms of cancer. The list of organs that can be damaged as a result of Chronic Fatigue Syndrome/Epstein-Barr virus are:

- Liver
- Spleen
- Thyroid gland
- Pancreas
- Adrenal glands

To illustrate how serious chronic fatigue is, I will tell you about a patient I am currently treating. "Lynn" is a young woman who is married and has two children. About a year ago, she was referred to me for supportive therapy and treatment of depression. She spent most of her day in bed or on the sofa and could barely make the drive to my office. She suffered from all of the symptoms previously mentioned but was having particular problems with migraines. Lynn had a happy marriage, wonderful daughters, and no financial concerns. My patient was highly motivated and willing to do whatever it took to regain her strength and former lifestyle. Her frequent hospitalizations for headaches were dragging her down.

Lynn enjoyed a happy childhood and maintained satisfying relationships with her family and friends. My patient had led a very active life, playing tennis and golf regularly, and she participated in school and civic activities. But all of these activities were now a thing of the past. She felt guilty about "not contributing to my family" and having to rely on her husband and other family members for assistance. All of her life she had been a "doer," and now just getting out of bed was almost an insurmountable task.

As if Lynn did not have enough problems, the internist, whom she saw to treat the chronic fatigue told her that he did not "believe" in the syndrome and that she needed to seek psychiatric care. Fortunately, the initial diagnosis came from a wonderful obstetrician–gynecologist. I was able to reassure Lynn that her feelings of depression were a symptom of what was happening to her, much like sneezing is a symptom of hay fever. She was actually responding to a trying situation appropriately. A change in internists was also reassuring and helpful.

There seems to be a relationship between a body insult and the E-B virus. Two years ago my patient had to undergo eye surgery, and, even though the procedure was successful, it was soon thereafter that she became ill with chronic fatigue.

Another patient that I am seeing shares a similar history. She had a hysterectomy, and, about a year later, she too was diagnosed with Chronic Fatigue Syndrome. Several other possible triggers are noteworthy. Keep in mind that it is the immune system that can be compromised by these factors.

Some possible triggers for activating the E-B Virus (CFS) and weakening the immune system are:

- Accidents
- Disease
- Old age
- Surgery
- Poor nutrition
- Overwhelming stress
- Substance abuse

Now, certainly, not everybody who has been beset by any of these ordeals develops Chronic Fatigue

Syndrome. If you do have feelings of extreme fatigue that seem quite debilitating, please see a physician immediately. There are other disorders that can cause fatigue so it is wise to be evaluated. And don't be afraid to ask questions. You need routine blood work as well as screening for the Epstein-Barr virus.

The two patients that I have mentioned are doing well. "Lynn" is still in the recovery phase and continues to make progress. My second patient has intermittent difficulties, but has adjusted her lifestyle accordingly. She maintains a full life—works, has a family, and sees friends—but when she begins to feel tired, she rests.

The course of chronic fatigue varies with the individual, much as mononucleosis does. Some people experience an initial challenging period of debilitating fatigue that lasts about two to five months, but over the next four to five months they improve, eventually regaining their old energy level. Others face a more formidable course.

Whether you have CFS or just lack energy, I have some suggestions that may be of merit. We shall begin with the "behavioral helpers" first, but of all of the disorders previously discussed in the earlier chapters, you may be surprised to see what an important role herbs play in CFS.

Behavioral Helpers

It is worth repeating—if you feel fatigued, like you have just climbed a mountain or run a marathon, and there does not seem to be a good reason, see your family doctor. With his or her approval you can begin a program to help you regain your strength. Initially, perhaps sleep is all you will be able to manage.

Steps to Healing CFS

Healing: Calm your mind with music, prayer, or meditation, books—whatever relaxes your body and spirit.

Exercise: Begin very slowly—yoga is excellent—then gradually increase your activity of choice.

Herbs: Your recovery period may be shortened by using the suggestions from "Herbs for Your Nerves."

Diet: Eliminate fatty and fried foods. Eat vegetables and fruit, whole grain cereal and bread, fish and chicken. Abstain from alcohol and nicotine.

Rest: Rest as much as necessary until you feel ready to begin a gradual exercise program. To garner the benefits of aromatherapy to help to rest, use a calming, soothing essential oil such as neroli or ylang-ylang.

Herbs for Your Nerves

Your immune system is under siege, which means that all systems are feeling the attack. Fighting back is imperative, and since there are no specific medications designed to "cure" Chronic Fatigue Syndrome, your approach needs to be to treat your symptoms and reinforce your immune system. Here's how.

Echinacea

Echinacea is listed in virtually every book on natural healing. Perhaps its greatest contribution has to do with its immune-enhancing effects, even though it has been used for abscesses, ulcers, and scarlet fever.

The complex sugar molecules known as polysaccharides stimulate the cells of the immune system. In addition, echinacea helps in the production of the interferons, which have a positive effect on infections caused by viruses.

The plant grows wild in North America and belongs to the sunflower family. It possesses a lovely purple blossom and is a favorite with wildflower fanciers.

For long-term usage, it should be taken for six to eight weeks at a time; then allow a break for four to six weeks and repeat the regimen. The root extract should be taken daily in the range of 900 milligrams in divided doses. The current *German Commission E Monograph* warns that people with lupus, tuberculosis, and multiple sclerosis should not use echinacea.

Turmeric

Turmeric is a spice used in traditional Indian cooking. In India, it is used to treat anorexia, cough, rheumatism, and even sinusitis. It helps to reduce swelling in recent bruises, wounds, and insect bites, and even helps treat head colds.

Turmeric has positive effects on the digestive, circulatory, and respiratory systems. It acts as a stimulant and antibacterial and may be helpful in treating Chronic Fatigue Syndrome. It also promotes a proper metabolism in the body and aids in the digestion of protein.

To use, take 1 to 2 grams per day in food or one capsule or tablet daily.

Caution: Turmeric is a strong dye and can stain clothes and furniture. Be advised when taking an herbal product such as turmeric; patience and repetitive use is required for results. There are no known side effects to turmeric.

◄ Reishi Mushroom ►

In Asia, the medicinal value of reishi mushrooms has long been recognized. In China, The mushroom has been used to treat wounds, inflammations, ulcers, and even cancer. In Japan, the reishi mushroom has been used for its anticancer abilities and support of the immune system.

In the United States, interest in the mushrooms has skyrocketed. It is now believed that the mushrooms may help enhance the immune system. the reishi mushroom is an "adaptagen," which is a substance that reduces the effects of stress and insomnia. The reishi mushroom is also effective in normalizing blood pressure, regulating the circulatory system, and treating Chronic Fatigue Syndrome.

To use, take 2 to 3 grams in capsule or tablet form, once a day.

◄ Astragalus ►

Some 2,000 years ago, astragalus was the herb of choice to increase energy levels and overcome fatigue. At M.D. Anderson Hospital and Turner Institute in Houston, Texas, researchers have been studying another property of astragalus, namely its ability to stimulate the immune system. But even more exciting, this herb may actually help *restore* the immune system.

Astragalus is a delicate little plant with small leaves. In China it is used extensively to also treat patients with diabetes, heart disease, and anemia. It is commonly used in tea form with one teaspoon of root to one and a half pints of water. It should be boiled in a covered pan for twenty to thirty minutes. Still covered, let it cool; drink one cup two times a day.

◄ Asian Ginseng (Panax) ►

At the beginning of our discussion regarding chronic fatigue, I mentioned that it seemed to be associated with, or possibly triggered by, traumas to the body such as surgery. Asian ginseng is one of those herbs that appears to be very helpful in recuperation and convalescence after a long illness or surgery. A talisman from China and Korea, it is a widely researched herb that also seems to have a "preventive medicine" quality, protecting the body against stress, common colds, and flu.

In Russia athletes are given Asian ginseng to hedge off fatigue and increase endurance. It is also given to geriatric patients, especially in Europe, to improve their ability to concentrate. One other intriguing fact about Asian ginseng is that it is prescribed in Germany and France to help maintain normal levels of blood sugar along with traditional treatment for diabetes.

Asian ginseng is a perennial that emits subtle, yellowish flowers that ultimately produce a small red berry. To have survived for more than 2,000 years, it had to be tough. Perhaps that may in part explain its preferred environment on rugged mountainsides in cold climates.

The recommended dose for Asian ginseng is 100 milligrams per day. Unfortunately, some people overuse it, which may cause nervousness, insomnia, and elevation in blood pressure. If you use ginseng, only take one type and only at the appropriate dose. This is one of those herbs that you take for several weeks and then skip two weeks before you resume the regimen.

◄ Licorice ►

Another herb that shows great promise for people suffering with CFS is licorice—and no, it's not exactly the same stuff we chewed on as kids. This herbal treat dates back to the ancient Greeks who used it for a variety of problems. The active ingredient that holds such promise is found in the root and is called glycyrrhizin. Research suggests that licorice holds anti-inflammatory as well as antiviral properties. Further, it has been demonstrated that glycyrrhizin actually inhibits the Epstein-Barr virus, the designated culprit associated with Chronic Fatigue Syndrome.

This herb has side effects that are very serious, however. They are dose-related and may occur when people ingest large quantities. **If you have heart problems or high blood pressure, you should not use this herb.** Licorice is often used to disguise the flavor of nasty tasting medications, but it poses no risk in very small amounts. Should you decide to use licorice, check with your doctor first.

Remember: Never use more than two or three herbs at a time, and *always* check it out with your family doctor first. Herbs can be very helpful if taken correctly and in the proper dosages.

Chapter 8
Memory

*Oh, better than the minting of a gold-crowned king
Is the safe-kept memory of a lovely thing.*
—Sara Teasdale, "The Coin," 1921

Memory loss is often associated with age, and, of course, the fear is that it heralds the onset of Alzheimer's, a disease that ultimately leads to total loss of memory. But nothing could be further from the truth. People between the ages of sixty-five and seventy-five are only at 4 to 10 percent risk of developing Alzheimer's, certainly a very low statistic. Folks in their twenties and thirties experience occasional bouts of memory problems such as forgetting where they put their keys, an appointment, a name, or an errand. But because of their age, they give little thought to the fear of memory loss. The same does not apply to people over forty. In your forties to sixties, if you forget your keys or struggle for a word, it is an automatic, but faulty assumption that you have Alzheimer's. Many factors figure into a brief lapse, such as not paying attention, worry, and the major contributor to poor memory—stress.

Walking down memory lane means taking a look at the brain and its billions of neurons or nerve cells. All of these neurons connect with other neurons and complete a maze of pathways that is the envy of all of your high-powered computers. As all new information is assimilated, our amazing brain sorts through, categorizes, and retains data that become stored in memory. It is true that as we age, some of our neurons whither and die, but we are talking about only a small number compared to the billions that we have. As one bites the dust, another takes its place. These neurons send out an electrical signal that produces a chemical change to another neuron and—voilà—memory.

At the turn of the nineteenth century, a researcher by the name of Franz Joseph Gall studied bumps on the head in an effort to link specific brain areas to specific faculties and personality traits. The idea of a localized specific area for memory was challenged in the 1900s by researchers like Karl

Lashley. He argued that memory was distributed equally throughout the brain. We now know that they were both correct.

Depending on the researcher, hypotheses about the brain vary widely. Many scientists hold that memory may be divided and identified by type such as semantic, implicit, remote, working, and episodic.

Semantic memory stores words and symbols and is probably the most lasting of the five. While people may forget specific incidences and even loved ones, they usually retain concepts such as what "clothes" or a "living room" means.

Implicit memories are associated with specific skills. You remember the phrase "just like riding a bicycle"? Well, it turns out that most people really do retain long-term knowledge of the skills needed to do such activities as riding a bike or swimming in a pool.

Remote memory allows you to access trivia and facts. As we age, there is a decline, but I can give you some behavioral helpers to help keep you sharp. The good news is, if you are older, you probably have amassed a lot of knowledge; the bad news—it's harder to retrieve. Be careful when you play Trivial Pursuit.

Your *working memory* tends to be very short term in duration. Suppose your supervisor is telling you about a job situation, but as you listen to your boss, you overhear another coworker while you peruse the mail. It's a bit like juggling—keeping all of those balls going at one time. How well you are able to do this and not become confused may not be just a function of age or stress, but rather intelligence.

Finally, *episodic memory* speaks to learning new material. For example, baby boomers have perhaps been more reticent to tackle the computer age than have our offspring who have embraced it with gusto. Nonetheless, episodic memory is the first to go.

Alzheimer's disease and other dementias gradually impair memory and rob the individual of their personality and essence. Dementia has upward of seventy causes, among them things we cannot control such as brain tumors and liver and kidney failure, but some things we can control, such as substance abuse and vitamin and nutritional deficiencies. Of the risk factors associated with dementia, age is the most robust, but genetic predispositions increase the odds three- to fourfold. Head injuries that leave you unconscious may also make you more vulnerable.

Patients with HIV/AIDS may be severely impacted by dementia as the virus attacks the white matter of the brain. Substance abuse, especially if chronic, causes degenerative changes in the brain. Researchers believe that one or two glasses of red wine a day may be beneficial, but levels that exceed such a number are harmful and catastrophic to memory. Depression, anxiety, obsessive-compulsive disorders, and post-traumatic stress disorder all can compromise cognitive abilities and thus memory. Alzheimer's has occasionally been misdiagnosed for depression.

Behavioral Helpers

I had the rare privilege of getting to know thirty or so prisoners of war from Vietnam. They were all pilots and all had been tortured. Their amazing stories of survival and faith will stay with me forever. Some of the men had been prisoners from five to eight years, spending two or three years in solitary confinement and in very small cages. Their memories were their only companion, and they maintained their sanity by "reteaching" themselves foreign languages, "rereading" books, and "writing" music. Sustained by their religious beliefs and memory, they survived by exercising their minds.

If you don't want to lose it, use it—and that seems to be the prevailing wisdom with memory. People who challenge themselves and never stop learning have fewer problems with their memory. They also, by the way, are happier.

Another trick is "association." If you want to remember a name or place, either come up with a rhyme or something that it is like. For example, I might want to remember a name such as "Bill Henderson." If the gentleman is from New York, I could associate his name with the Buffalo Bills that do not want to be "hindered" in their Super Bowl goal. A rhyme could be: "Bill Henderson is slender-son."

And, of course, there are mnemonics. If you want a thumbnail sketch of herbs, it becomes:

HELP

- Health
- Energy
- Longevity
- Plentiful

Visualization is another way to access memory by actively picturing in your mind an image prompt. For example, if you want to remember someone's name, you select a prominent feature of the person. Get the name, transform the name to the image, and then link the image of the name to the prominent feature. A word of caution: Be careful about the image!

Herbs for Your Nerves

◄ Ginkgo Biloba ►

It comes from the oldest tree on the earth, dating back to the dinosaur era some 200 million years ago. Its existence spans the ages and grew first in North America and Europe until the Ice Age. It is revered in Oriental medicine and is an invaluable treatment for memory loss. This venerable herb seems to increase circulation to the brain. It also yields a protective effect on nerve cells, and recent studies suggest that ginkgo biloba may help regenerate damaged nerve cells as a result of the terpene lactones found in it.

Perhaps because it is the oldest herb known to man, this senior tree has also been the best researched. It was initially thought to be helpful with respiratory ailments, but quite quickly its spectrum widened to include use for circulation problems such as impotence, depression, and memory. These latter disorders are all intricately linked to blood flow in the body and brain. Supported by no less than 400 research studies, it is not surprising how widely prescribed this herb has become.

In one study, thirty-one patients all over the age of fifty were given ginkgo biloba. Each participant had previously experienced moderate memory impairment, but after only six months, it was demonstrated that mental efficiency was improved.

Ginkgo biloba is seemingly without any side effects, and the current *German Commission E Monograph* lists no contraindications. The standardized dose of 120 to 160 milligrams in two or three divided doses does the trick. You need to be patient because it may take a while to kick in.

In the meantime, don't forget to take your ginkgo biloba!

◄ Phosphatidylserine ►

After decades of research and peer review, scientists have blessed the efficacy of an amazing little substance with a very funny name.

Phosphatidylserine (or PS) can be found in every cell in the body, and when you take into consideration that there are some 200 billion cells, that is a remarkable thought. At the cellular level, PS is an essential building block in the brain. In a very sophisticated and complex fashion, PS works on nerve cells in the brain, connecting, revitalizing, rebuilding, and integrating.

In Alzheimer's and other forms of dementia, patients not only lose their memory, but they also have compromised cognitive skills. Everyday tasks such as eating, getting dressed, or using the bathroom are lost. Studies show that when given PS, some patients with Alzheimer's and other forms of dementia may actually have a reversal of some symptoms. Other studies demonstrate that PS is very effective in dealing with people who are under a great deal of stress. Further, PS is associated with improvements in depression as well as improvements in performance for athletes.

As a dietary supplement, PS appears to be quite safe and appropriate for all adults regardless of their age. If you want to include PS as a dietary supplement, it is suggested that you begin with a slightly higher dose of 200 to 300 milligrams per day with meals and then go to a maintenance level, which would be about 100 to 200 milligrams daily.

◄ Other Substances ►

There is some indication in the professional literature that perhaps NSAIDs, nonsteroidal, anti-inflammatory drugs such as aspirin or ibuprofen, may be beneficial as well. Perhaps as little as half of a recommended dose for either of the two drugs mentioned taken daily does the trick.

Remember: Never use more than two or three herbs at a time, and *always* check it out with your family doctor first. Herbs can be very helpful if taken correctly and in the proper dosages.

Chapter 9
Sexuality

Nobody ever won the battle of the sexes. There is too much fraternizing with the enemy.
—*Dr. Henry A. Kissinger*

One of the most magnificent gifts is the physical love between two people. This sacred union has been the inspiration for poets, musicians, artists, and storytellers.

Part of being human is our ability to express the love we feel for others. We can trace man's search for intimacy through oral traditions and early writings. This exquisite communication has now become a science in part to garner an understanding of the intricate link between our bodies and our minds, but further, it elucidates the mechanics that can improve intimate expression.

What if I were to tell you there are ways to increase your sexual desire and your sexual abilities? What if I could suggest to you that there may even be ways to improve a man's erection and, for older lovers, to help promote a healthier prostate? Would you be skeptical or adventurous? If you are the skeptic, then I encourage you to investigate the following remedies for yourself. And if you're the adventurer, you might be in for some nice surprises.

It is wise to mention that human sexuality is a booming business and can lead to exploitation. Advertisements that make outrageous claims regarding "cures" should be scrupulously evaluated and probably avoided. Make certain that there are reliable scientific studies to support the usage of a product. *Always talk to your physician prior to ingesting any substance.*

With sex comes responsibility. Making certain that all necessary precautions are taken minimizes the risks of disease or pregnancy.

Achieving great intimacy is about mutual love and respect. A corollary is maintaining a healthy body and lifestyle. People can expect to enjoy lovemaking well into their old age and can experience a sense of fulfillment. The mutual expression of commitment and love is a joyful treasure at any age. It truly enhances the quality of life.

Aphrodisiacs and Vitality

It is only recently that modern medicine has looked at the significance of vitamins, minerals, herbs, and spices to achieve good health and lasting sexuality. It turns out that the answer to an improved sex life may only be as far away as your neighborhood health food store and grocer. If you speak to any athlete, they will tell you the importance of proper nutrition, vitamins, and minerals as part of getting into peak condition. They will also be quick to point out that their performance is only as good as their physical condition. They may tell you that practice improves their skills and abilities—and so is the case with lovemaking. Great performance is fundamentally connected to your physical health and your willingness to practice.

In the past, traditional medicine has overlooked the importance of what some ancients had to say about aphrodisiacs. Aphrodisiacs are substances that when ingested are touted to improve sexual arousal, desire, and ability in both men and women.

Almost every culture claims to have great aphrodisiacs, but what are they and do they work? It depends on whom you ask. Aphrodisiacs are restorative foods, herbs, and spices, along with nutritional supplements, that are believed to actively manipulate your brain into thinking amorous thoughts.

Herbs for Your Nerves—Vitality

◄ Chocolate ►

Chocolate and cocoa, the dark bitter variety, is a love food. From its sensual smell to its delicious taste, chocolate seduces its object of love. It contains sugar, caffeine, and theobromine, all of which increase digestive secretions and dilate blood vessels that promote flow to the penis for erection and to the vagina. This central nervous stimulant was recognized by ancient Meso-American Indians as an aphrodisiac. They believed the cocoa beans contained the secret to sexual enticement. Montezuma, the great Aztec leader, used a formula of dark cocoa, hot water, honey, and vanilla. (You don't want to use milk because milk will put you to sleep!) He would concoct this delicious brew before he made love. Rumors attesting to his prowess were etched in stone.

◄ Honey ►

Honey, another love food, is the fastest absorbed food that the body can draw on for energy. When using honey, you need to use the darkest form. It naturally replenishes one's energy and allows lovemaking to go on and on. Now you know why the first week of marriage is often referred to as the honeymoon!

◄ Royal Jelly ►

Royal jelly, which you can buy in capsule form in the health food store, is a rich source of pantathetic acid. In combination with vitamin C, pantathetic acid activates the adrenal glands, which give us energy to engage in frequent lovemaking.

◄ Lecithin ►

Lecithin is a concentrated virility food that may increase a woman's desire or a man's libido. It, too, can be purchased in a health food store. When you take lecithin, make sure that it is standardized to contain 35 percent choline so that your brain gets the powerful nutrition it needs.

◄ Caviar ►

Caviar was a favorite of Catherine the Great, whose sexual desires are legendary. The Chinese agreed with the Russian queen but added bird's nest soup to the mix. Caviar is fish eggs any way you look at it, so perhaps its aphrodisiac potential resides in the protein. So feel free to eat all the caviar you can afford!

◄ Seeds and Nuts ►

Seeds and nut fruits are used to produce plant life, but our bodies can benefit from them as well. Pumpkin seeds can help a declining prostate. Taken with zinc, it becomes a virility food, which assists the body in stimulating glandular production. Walnuts, Brazil nuts, and pistachios in combination with raisins and apricots can be used in salads and in cereals to help energize you.

◄ Onions and Garlic ►

Onions and garlic are a good news/bad news situation. The good news is that onions and garlic, eaten prior to lovemaking, may promote energy stamina. The bad news is, of course, bad breath, a downside worth consideration.

◄ Vitamins ►

We cannot conclude our discussion on aphrodisiacs and vitality supplements without focusing on the contribution of vitamins. A word of warning: Vitamins should be taken according to FDA daily requirement dosages. Excess amounts of vitamins and minerals can be dangerous and even toxic.

Eating Healthy

Hippocrates, who was the father of modern medicine and a great teacher, once observed that food is medicine and medicine is food, even though he lacked the fundamental knowledge that today's children learn in school regarding food groups and the science behind it. His intellectual curiosity laid the groundwork for nutrition and pharmaceuticals.

The importance of eating a diet rich in fruits and raw vegetables cannot be overemphasized. Our bodies are complex machines that must have the appropriate nutritional formula in order to function optimally.

Your local health food store can be a valuable resource of both products and information about different herbal or food product remedies. I encourage you to experiment with some of the suggestions I mentioned. And, as a follow-up, there are many books available that give recipes for foods that may increase and add enjoyment to your love life. One excellent reference that I have used in this section is *New Power to Love* by William H. Lee, Ph.D.

Libido

Perhaps the single most difficult concern that doctors assist patients with in sex therapy is lack of libido. It occurs both in men and women and is not necessarily age-related. Low sexual desire has been the fodder of many comedians, but in a relationship it is anything but funny. An old rule of thumb is that the person with the lowest libido controls the marriage. There are a variety of reasons to explain this problem—psychodynamics, culture, sexual abuse, disease, lack of information about sexual intimacy, religious issues, and drugs are among them.

Positive therapeutic outcomes are not easily achieved and become impossible if the couple no longer love each other. Assuming this is not the case, Masters and Johnson developed a technique that they refer to as sensate focus. Briefly, the couple is first evaluated for any underlying diseases, and then they are given instructions to be carefully followed. It is a gradual process that begins with gentle touching, and, over a period of weeks, a rekindling of loving desire results in coitus. Sometimes people lose their way with each other and drift apart; sensate focus reminds a couple why they married each other in the first place.

Often related to a busy and demanding lifestyle or middle age, the level of the male hormone testosterone in a man or woman may drop significantly. Unfortunately, this decrease may cause a dramatic lessening of libido. Sometimes referred to as the "love hormone," testosterone replacement therapy can jump-start a stressed or tired engine. Research demonstrates that the administration of testosterone increases sexual drive, fantasy, and function. Your personal physician is the person to turn to and will guide you through the replacement process.

Putting the Spark Back into Marriage

You have been married to the same person for the past seven to fifteen to twenty years. You are in a rut. The relationship is stagnant, and you may be getting signals from your mate that he or she is feeling bored and disinterested. The spark has gone, communication is poor, and sex is business as usual, that is, when you even have sex. Maybe you find yourself daydreaming about the old days or fantasizing about others.

Suddenly, there doesn't seem to be as much reason for staying in the marriage as there once was. For women who have stayed at home, there may be a role loss—the kids just don't need Mom too much these days. For men, it heralds the peak of their business or professional career and often a midlife crisis. It's a time when you become more aware of your age and the time you have left to live. Then comes menopause and being a grandparent. Both men and women react to this new stage in life, and it can be a time when marriages really feel the stress of the years spent together.

So how does one go about taking the ho-hum out of a relationship and creating more excitement and fulfillment? First understand that changes in sexual behavior occur very gradually over the years. Mutual or individual boredom is quite often an issue, but the second most common reason is that after all this time, you have become sexually, erotically, and emotionally desensitized to one another.

The relationship is just no longer very exciting. Some people will tell you that this is normal—don't worry, just accept it—but don't believe that. In psychology we call the following technique "acting as if." Take a look at the behavior of young lovers, how they love each other with their entire bodies while being fully clothed and in public. They make love with their eyes, hold hands, and pay attention to what one or the other is saying. They listen, they question. Imitate some of these behaviors with your spouse.

Do things in a different fashion. Make a date to meet each other at a motel where it is quiet, private, and relaxing. Get a sex manual or movie to teach you some variations in lovemaking. Read or watch it together and talk about it. Understand that sex is 90 percent emotional and 10 percent physical.

Sleep in the nude. Shower together and recreate some of the intimacy that has been missing. Share and discuss life's daily happenings in order to promote a greater sense of intimacy.

Herbs for Your Nerves—Libido

◄ Wild Yams ►

The delicate pale yellowish flower perched on a long vine belies the lofty properties of this decorative plant. Wild yam is a hearty perennial found both in the north and the south. It survives the ravages of a Minnesota winter and a baking in the hot Texas sun. Oral tradition tells us it was used by Southern slaves to treat rheumatism, perhaps due to its anti-inflammatory benefits. The plant contains diosgenin, an element that converts to progesterone.

◄ Dehydro-epiandro-sterone (DHEA) ►

DHEA is a natural body hormone that is produced in the adrenal glands and to a lesser degree in the ovaries. I will discuss DHEA more fully in the chapter on antiaging, but suffice it to say that DHEA positively impacts the autoimmune system, skin, muscle, and bone, and reduces the risk of breast cancer that is associated with hormonal replacement therapy. DHEA is produced by plant sterole (our friend, the wild yam) through chemical synthesis and can be found as a food supplement in health food stores. Always consult your physician before taking DHEA. The lowest dose to be used when one begins DHEA therapy ranges from 10 to 25 milligrams each day. Doses that exceed 25 milligrams are not recommended.

◄ *Epimedium grandiflorum* ►

Epimedium grandiflorum (commonly known as bishop's hat) is a hearty plant that can be found in rock gardens or wild gardens. It succeeds in any fertile, humus-rich soil and grows best in semi-shade. The plants can also thrive in the dry shade of trees. They are hardy, although the flowers in spring can be damaged by late frosts. Members of this genus are rarely if ever troubled by grazing deer or rabbits.

While *Epimedium grandiflorum* can be found in gardens, more recently attention has been paid to its medicinal properties. It produces higher dopamine levels, which in turn result in higher levels of testosterone. Current findings regarding epimedium show that it heightens the sensitivity of nerve endings, which may affect sexual stimulation. Claims state that it can help lift your libido, restore sexual vigor, stimulate sensory nerves, and ignite the flame of passion. Further, it can fortify the kidneys and sperm and increases blood circulation to help remove obstructions and promote the flow of vital energy by regulating internal and hormonal functions to improve overall sexual virility and potency.

◄ Motherwort ►

Motherwort can be found in the northern part of the United States and all over Europe. It is a sturdy plant that can be found in vineyards and along fences and paths. During the Middle Ages, motherwort was used to cure fainting spells and other symptoms of nervousness or weakness as a result of excitement or illness. Some people even used the herb to protect against evil spirits. Some used it for certain heart maladies, and still others said it gladdens the heart and mind.

Native Americans, such as the Delaware, Micmac, Modeheman, and Shinecock tribes, used motherwort to treat gynecological disorders. Named for its use in treating symptoms relating to female reproductive disorders, motherwort is said to invigorate blood and promote urination.

To use motherwort, put one teaspoon in one cup of boiling water. Unless otherwise prescribed, the daily dosage should not exceed 4.5 grams of the cut herb. **Caution:** Motherwort is not recommended for use during pregnancy. There are no other known side effects or contraindications.

Men's Issues

Sexual Issues and Concerns

Senator Robert Dole is a very brave man. As a soldier and a statesman, his courage is well documented. But he is also to be commended and admired for talking openly about a very personal problem—erectile dysfunction (ED), or impotence. His leadership and candor has made it possible for other men with the same problem to talk openly with their doctor and get some help.

Impotence is linked to many culprits, among them such diseases as diabetes, hypertension, and heart disease. Other causes of impotence may be substance abuse, stress, poor nutrition, medication, hormones, trauma, and aging. We used to believe that 75 percent of erectile dysfunction was related to our emotional state. Not so, according to research. Even though impotence may cause alarm and embarrassment, what is important is that today almost every man can be helped.

In young men, impotence caused by psychological problems, such as anger, depression, and low self-esteem, is more common. Erectile dysfunction can wreak havoc in a marriage, resulting in intimacy problems. In older men, impotence is generally related to disease, hormones, or the general decline associated with age.

Modern medicine offers the most appropriate choices for men who suffer from moderate to severe ED. For some men, modern drug therapy and perhaps even surgical intervention that may include implants may be warranted. Either alone or in conjunction with medication, sex therapy can significantly improve sexual dysfunction through proven techniques, information, and psychotherapy.

There's a lot of hope out there.

If erectile dysfunction is transient, meaning it comes and goes, nontraditional treatment can perhaps be helpful. Such a treatment regime would include, but is not limited to, herbal solutions.

Herbs for Your Nerves—Men

Kola

Kola caffeine comes to us in the form of a small bean, nut, or seed, which grows on both trees and plants. Caffeine is a strong stimulant that can increase the heart rate and may, in turn, increase the flow of blood to the penis.

Guaraná

Guaraná is another plant form of caffeine and is highly concentrated, containing two and a half times more caffeine than coffee. Medicinally, the Brazilian Indians have also used it in the treatment of neuralgia, paralysis, and urinary tract infections. One teaspoon of guaraná is placed in one cup of sweetened water and then stirred and swallowed. If nothing else occurs, you will definitely be staying awake.

Damiana

Damiana is a sunny little shrub that may be found in California, Mexico, and South America. It enjoys the reputation of being a safe aphrodisiac as well as a treatment for impotency. Unlike many herbs whose medicinal value is contained in the roots, the leaves hold the magic. The recommended dose is 800 milligrams three times daily.

Yohimbe

Yohimbe is a controversial herb that has been on the U.S. FDA unsafe herb list since March 1977. I mention this herb as a warning. Research suggests that one would have to consume a megadose to have the desired result of dilation of genital blood vessels. Such a dose would cause toxicity and would not have value in resolving impotency. This herb has been popular and is well known, but it is extremely dangerous. You don't want to take it for fear of the outcome.

Sarsaparilla

Sarsaparilla is a delightful little vine that winds its way up and around other bushes, trees, or whatever is near it. Native Americans used the root of the vine for a variety of ailments including coughs, fever, kidney problems, and syphilis. This plant seems to possess some hormonal products, which, in the case of impotence due primarily to age and stress, may improve testosterone levels. Recent findings suggest that sarsaparilla is a mild diuretic and may assist the body in ridding itself of uric acid. To use sarsaparilla, take one teaspoon of the root and add one and a half pints of water, bring it to a boil, cover, and allow the liquid to cool. Make sure you keep the cover on while it is cooling. You can then drink up to one cup daily.

Saw Palmetto

Native American tribes used the berries of the saw palmetto to treat problems relating to the genitals, urinary tract, and reproductive system. Saw palmetto is also widely used in various parts of Europe and the United States for producing positive effects on the prostate and also as an aphrodisiac. Take 585 milligrams two times each day.

In men, saw palmetto benefits an enlarged and weakened prostate gland. It prevents testosterone from converting into dihydrotestosterone, the hormone thought to be responsible for the multiplication of the prostate cells and enlarging the prostate.

To use, eat the fresh berries or the dried berries in capsule form. The tea form of saw palmetto produces little or no results. Caution: Do not use during pregnancy or during lactation. Stomach problems and headaches are known side effects. Large amounts of the berries may cause diarrhea.

Tribulus terresteris

Tribulus terresteris, also known as the puncture vine, has long been used in Eastern parts of the world to stimulate hormone production and improve strength and stamina. Its first known recording in history dates back to 700 B.C., when Charaka, an Ayurvedic physician, described tribulus as a diuretic and aphrodisiac.

The effects of tribulus stem from its ability to produce higher levels of dopamine in the brain.

Higher levels of dopamine stimulate the production of testosterone that positively affects strength, libido, and sperm production.

Research studies on men, aged twenty-eight to forty-five, produced 30 percent higher levels of testosterone when taken in three doses of 250 milligrams for five days. To use, take 250 to 750 milligrams daily in even doses or as prescribed by a physician. Caution: *Tribulus terresteris* should not be taken by pregnant women or by children or by anyone with psychosis or schizophrenia. It should not be mixed with any other medications such as sedatives, tranquilizers, stimulants, and antidepressants. These medications include any over-the-counter medications.

Women's Issues

Premenstrual Syndrome (PMS)

Premenstrual Syndrome (PMS) is a collection of most unwanted symptoms that announce the onset of menses. Bloating, irritability, cramping, increased appetite, and anxiety may occur a week or ten days prior to menstruation and can be quite debilitating. It is recommended that a woman, a few days prior to the presentation of symptoms, eat five to six small meals each day. These meals should be rich in vitamins, minerals, and iron. A low-fat diet, heavy on whole grains and vegetables along with sodium restriction, may reduce water retention and general discomfort.

Many women find that a balanced diet and healthy snacks are helpful in combating PMS, as are avoiding caffeine and reducing salt intake. Stress reduction methods and daily exercise may also offer relief.

Along with diet, exercise is an integral part of PMS management. It may seem that grabbing a heating pad and lying down on the sofa in front of the television is a great idea, but research on PMS says it is not. A body in motion stimulates the natural production of morphine and thus reduces cramps. If you are not up for an aerobic workout, maybe taking a walk or doing another mild form of aerobic activity may be the answer.

◄ Angelica ►

In western parts of the world, angelica has been used for centuries. Often found in well-watered mountain ravines or damp meadows, angelica was once worn in necklace form to protect children from illness and witchcraft. Angelica, according to legend, is so named because a monk dreamed an angel told him that the herb could cure the Bubonic Plague. Due to the disastrous effects of the plague in Western Europe, angelica lost favor as a healing herb.

More recently, the popularity of Chinese angelica *(Angelica sinensis)* has regained favor for its medicinal purposes. Chinese angelica, also known as dong quai, is used for gynecological health. It is an all-purpose herb that has been used for centuries in

China to ease painful menstrual cramps and to eliminate the discomfort often associated with PMS.

To use Chinese angelica, make a medicinal tea of one teaspoon of crushed root per one cup of boiling water. Steep for ten to twenty minutes. It is also available in tablet form (0.5 grams of the extract); take twice daily. **Caution:** Do not use Chinese angelica during pregnancy. Hypersensitivity to the herb may cause excessive bleeding and occasional fever. It may also have a mild laxative effect.

◄ Chaste Tree ►

The chaste tree has long been used for a variety of medical reasons and the seeds were once said to have helped a virtuous person remain "chaste." Athenian women would string the leaves along their couches during the sacred rites of Cerces.

Native to the Mediterranean basin, the effects of the chaste tree lie in the normalization process of women's hormones. The tree is able to restore a normal estrogen-progesterone balance. It is also said to cure the symptoms of PMS, especially if the symptoms dissipate with the onset of menstruation.

Clinical studies supporting these findings were done in Germany. The trials of over 1,500 women found that one-third of the patients experienced resolved PMS symptoms and 57 percent of the patients reported significant improvement of their symptoms. Overall, 90 percent reported improvement or complete resolution of their PMS symptoms.

The useful parts of the tree are the peppercorn-like purple berries it produces. To use the chaste tree berries, put forty drops of concentrated liquid per glass of water; drink in the morning. It is also available in powdered form, via tablets and capsules; use 175 to 225 milligrams daily. Possible side effects: stomach upset, mild skin rash, headache, or nausea. It is not recommended for use during pregnancy.

Pregnancy

One of the biggest challenges women face during pregnancy often appears in the first trimester: morning sickness. Of course, as many women will attest, "morning" sickness may occur in the afternoon, evening, or at night. Unfortunately some women experience nausea all day long. Since nausea is correlated with hypoglycemia, maintaining a level blood sugar is imperative. Having small snacks throughout the day is the wisest route, as well as avoiding food with quick-absorbing sugars. However, these remedies alone often do not curb the nausea for many women. With the support of your gynecologist, natural treatments may be sought.

◄ Ginger Root *(Zingiber officinale)* ►

This herb has been successful in vomit prevention and controlling nausea. The root is the only part of the plant to have medicinal properties.

Ginger root may be prepared in tea, or for a stronger dose, 2 grams of powdered ginger root with a bit of liquid is useful.

Ginger is indigenous to southeast Asia, but was brought to America in the fifteenth century. The Chinese have used ginger root for controlling asthma, water retention, diarrhea, gas release, and appetite loss. Asian medicine has used the root for centuries in treating nausea and vomiting.

◄ Ignatia ►

A homeopathic remedy, ignatia taken in small doses several times a day may ease nausea associated with the sight and smell of food.

◄ Black Haw *(Viburnum prunifolium)* ►

As a woman's pregnancy progresses, nausea often subsides, but new concerns rise. Black haw is commonly used to support women with disorders in their reproductive organs. Cramping caused by contractions in pelvic muscles may be relieved with the use of black haw. Midwives have used it to calm an irritable womb for the purpose of impeding a miscarriage.

Black haw is a member of the honeysuckle family. It is indigenous to our country but can be found in South America, Asia, and Europe, flowering from March through June. The black haw leaves are often used for tea, and it is helpful as an astringent for diarrhea and dysentery.

◄ Hammamelis ►

Due to physical changes in the second trimester of pregnancy, women often experience leg cramps and heaviness. This is a result of decreased vein contractions, increased blood volume, impeded blood circulation, and a decline of physical exercise. While walking will improve circulation, hammamelis, a homeopathic remedy taken several times a day, is helpful.

◄ Blue Cohosh *(Caulophyllum thalictroides)* ►

Found growing in rich, moist soil, blue cohosh is used as an antispasmodic and a diuretic. It is beneficial to women before childbirth because it relaxes the uterus. Soaking one ounce of blue cohosh root in one pint of boiling water for thirty minutes and drinking two to four fluid ounces several times a day is recommended as the expected day of delivery nears.

◄ Black Cohosh *(Cimicifuga racemosa)* ►

This root is commonly known as black cohosh, but also may be found under the name of black snake root, bugbane, bugwort, rattle root, richweed, or squaw root. For medicinal purposes, only the root has been successful. A native to the United States and Canada, black cohosh has been used to ease premenstrual discomfort and painful menses. Because the root exhibits an effect concordant to estrogen, menopausal women may use it. Black cohosh has been effective in controlling the discomfort of postpartum bleeding due to its anti-inflammatory and sedative properties.

◄ Shepherd's Purse *(Capsella bursa-pastoris)* ►

As a member of the mustard family, shepherd's purse is used in a variety of culinary dishes. The leaves may be cooked or used in salads and the seeds used for peppery seasoning or meal ground. The leaves are a good source for beta-carotene, iron, calcium, riboflavin, potassium, and ascorbic acid. The entire plant including flowers is used for medicinal purposes as an astringent and diuretic. Pregnant women should not use shepherd's purse, but it is beneficial after childbirth for postpartum bleeding; it also can aid in contracting the uterus once the child has been born.

◄ Bilberry ►

Both the leaves and the berries of this small green shrub have been used to ease the symptoms of a variety of illnesses from funguses, yeasts, and bacteria. But for pregnant women, it has been especially beneficial to prevent hemorrhoids. During the third trimester, babies gain a disproportionate amount of weight. With the combination of the baby's weight gain and gravity, a great deal of pressure is exerted, and expectant moms find themselves having to deal with yet another problem—hemorrhoids.

With the use of bilberry, capillary fragility is reduced and so fewer varices or other blood problems occur. Researchers have found no problems associated with bilberry given along with vitamin E in the last trimester of pregnancy. However, it should not be used in the first two trimesters. A maintenance dose of 240 milligrams taken daily seems to do the trick.

Sexual Desire

Women are often ashamed and embarrassed to admit having sexual difficulty, yet virility is just as important to women. Pregnancy and menopause are unique to the female gender. These are times in a woman's life of increased anxiety and moodiness due to the hormonal changes occurring in the body. Although nothing can replace being under the care of a trained physician, understanding what herbs may soothe the sensations of changes is helpful. Correct use of natural elements combined with the support and comfort from family and friends may ease the discomfort.

Women often feel a lag in sexual desire due to a variety of reasons such as fatigue, age, motherhood, illness, and other factors. Instead of giving up, herbal remedies may be just what is needed to get a spark back into a romantic life.

◄ Golden Root *(Scutellaria baicalensis)* ►

The Chinese and Japanese have used golden root for treatment of inflammation. Western science has seen the success and uses the root for respiratory infections, liver disorders, hypertension, insomnia, diarrhea, dysentery, and inflammation. Research using animals has verified the local inflammation-reducing properties of this root. Scientists are examining the benefits of golden root in treating HIV infections.

Golden root has been successful in increasing sexual desire. It can be found in tablet form, or the roots can be boiled in hot water. Six to fifteen grams a day is typically sufficient.

◄ Asian Ginseng ►

Ginseng acts as a hormone balancer and thus relieves menopausal symptoms. There is also a belief that it may reduce the risk of breast cancer, osteoporosis, and even heart disease. Additional properties may contribute to the prevention of the thinning of the vaginal walls and vaginal dryness. The recommended dosage is 200 milligrams four times a day.

◄ Herbal Teas ►

If you are blessed enough to live in Texas, you probably drink tea at dinnertime. Teas generally come in two categories: black tea, which is most common in Western countries, and green tea, which is enjoyed more commonly in the Orient. Of the two, green tea is more therapeutic because it contains twice as much vitamin C as black tea and twice the amount of catechins. Clinical investigations seem to support that green teas may help to prevent some forms of cancer and delay the development of arteriosclerosis. Because of the polyphenols, the immune system becomes more efficient, which may explain the antiviral property. Green tea is effective for a plethora of problems from dysentery to mental fatigue.

Menopause

Menopause, often referred to as "the change of life," is a normal phase that can be both liberating and exciting. The process can span many years and may begin in the mid-forties. The body gradually reduces the amount of estrogen released from the ovaries. While there may indeed be some less-than-pleasant side effects that herald the onset of menopause, most symptoms can be resolved naturally for many women.

Traditionally, the onset of menopause begins when the last child gets packed off to college. And with no more kids to rear, a woman is free to pursue any adventure she may wish—a career beginning or career change, having more fun volunteering, furthering her education, or self-exploration are at last possible. Perhaps one of the most beneficial aspects of completing menopause is sexual freedom. Worries about birth control are a thing of the past. Now making love has more to do with closeness, emotional intimacy, physical pleasure, and a rebonding of old promises.

There is a lot of debate in the literature regarding hormonal replacement therapy during and after menopause. Some women breeze naturally through menopause, but others battle such intrusive and undesirable symptoms as hot flashes, insomnia, fatigue, irritability, and low libido. One must judiciously weigh the pros and cons of taking hormonal replacement therapy with their physician. The benefits and risks involved in hormonal replacement therapy can be confusing. The research on osteoporosis and heart disease cannot be dismissed, but neither can the research on cancer. The only way to make informed decisions is through careful consultation.

There are some strategies for coping with menopause that will help all women regardless of symptoms. Seeking medical support is always important. Yearly physical exams including pelvic exams, Pap smears, mammograms, and colon checks are essential. Diet and exercise are equally significant in combating the side effects of menopause. A diet rich in soy will help decrease hot flashes as well as improve overall health. Exercise will help maintain a healthy weight, lower stress, increase energy, and improve your sleep. Another wise strategy is to end your bad habits. Smoking, alcohol, and too much caffeine often increase the occurrence of hot flashes. Finally, talk and laugh with girlfriends about your struggles with menopause. A sense of humor will help ease the pangs of change, and friendships will offer support and understanding. Sharing with a friend who has experienced menopause is often comforting.

Chapter 10
Aging

*As a white candle
In a holy place,
So is the beauty
Of an aged face.*

—*Joseph Campbell*

Wish that we might, eternal life is not realistic; however, slowing down the aging process is an obtainable goal. As baby boomers enter middle age the fear of growing old has prompted researchers to find ways to reduce the effects of aging. Changing the aging process is possible through diet, exercise, and tension reduction.

Diet

Although fast food is the "American way," maintaining a healthy diet will certainly help us to age gracefully. As the body ages, physical strength is reduced, posture becomes poor, digestion can be difficult, skins loses its elasticity and may become discolored and dry, and serious diseases become more prevalent. Not a pretty picture! Perhaps the biggest fear is senility. Fortunately there are vitamins and other supplements that can help us as we go down life's inevitable path.

In addition to establishing a healthy diet, with all food groups represented, supplements are extremely beneficial to one's health. Vitamins, minerals, carotenoids, and replenishing hormones may slow down the aging process. Adding supplements to the diet will promote metabolic functions, increase antioxidant activity, and detoxify harmful elements.

To begin with, we all need a multivitamin that provides B-complex, vitamins C and E, and beta-carotene. Trace minerals, calcium, and magnesium that may be found in a multivitamin are valuable assets.

B-complex vitamins provide many useful qualities. Vitamin B_2 (riboflavin) facilitates the transformation of amino acids into neurotransmitters. Vitamin B_3 (niacinamide) impacts effective functioning of the nervous system. Vitamin B_{12} can help with insomnia and anemia; it also influences psychological and neurological functioning.

Vitamin C is a protective antioxidant, which increases immunity, promotes wound healing, and enhances collagen production. This vitamin protects us against cancer, heart disease, and oxidative damage. Vitamin C is also helpful in curtailing the common cold. In fact, some studies show that a dose of 500 milligrams four times a day can lessen the length of cold symptoms by half. Check with your doctor first. I don't recommend this dose.

Vitamin E also protects us against cancer and heart disease, and perhaps diabetic retinopathy and kidney disease. Vitamin E boosts the immune system by enhancing white blood cells. Finally, vitamin E may delay wrinkle development. Some research even shows that applying vitamin E in liquid form to wrinkles may be useful.

Carotenoids, such as beta-carotene, protect against heart disease and cancer. The most prevalent carotenoid found in our blood is lycopene. Perhaps high levels of lycopene can impede prostate cancer. Lycopene has also been found to protect against age-related macular degeneration, an eye disease.

Minerals, such as iron, are instrumental in fighting age-related problems by increasing antioxidant enzymes produced in the body. Manganese and copper are also beneficial in enhancing antioxidant enzymes. Zinc is an important mineral known to have declining levels as we grow older. Decreased zinc levels lead to lower immunity. By taking zinc, we may build and improve our T-cell functioning, which may result in improved immunity.

Exercise

As we age, it is vital to keep our muscles in good shape because we tend to lose muscle strength as time passes. Not all exercise has to be rigorous; aerobic exercise a few times a week is extremely necessary. At the very least we need to stretch our muscles, and doing so should be a part of our daily routine to impede the aging process.

Stretching your back can help prevent back pain. By standing up and pressing the palms of your hands on your lower back for support you can gently arch your back. Hold the position and then release, relaxing your muscles. Doing this fifteen to twenty times a day can strengthen your back.

Shoulder rolls help reduce tension on the upper back and neck. They will limber shoulders, improve posture, and provide relief from arthritic stiffness. Simply standing with your arms at your side, let your arms dangle loosely. Lift both shoulders up toward your ears and roll them in a circular motion forward, down, and back. Repeat this fifteen to twenty times a day.

The standing reach is an aid for improving balance. Standing with your arms at your sides, fix your eyes on a spot on the wall in order to keep your balance. Now, breathe out, and as you breathe in, raise your arms in a wide circle to your sides and touch over your head. Come up on your toes during this process and hold your breath while reaching gently to the ceiling.

Finally, breathe out while bringing your arms slowly down to the starting position. You should lower your heels to the floor at the same time. The standing reach will not only help with balance, but limber your shoulder joints, expand the rib cage, and strengthen your ankles and calves.

The squat stretch will strengthen the back of your legs, limber the lower back, and stretch the chest muscles. Begin with your feet parallel, but a few inches apart. Bend your knees slightly and clasp your hands with your elbows resting on your knees. With your head lifted slightly, breathe in, and as you breathe out, tuck your head and straighten your legs. Keep your elbows to your knees. Do this five to ten times a day. Most professional trainers believe that mild weight lifting is essential. Weight training adds tone and strength to the body and to the muscles.

The diaphragm breathe is good not only for stretching your abdominal muscles, but also for relaxation. In a comfortable seated position, place both hands on your stomach just under your navel, and exhale while contracting your stomach muscle. You can push in with your hands to teach your body how to do the exercise. Then relax your abdomen and inhale, pushing your hands forward with your stomach muscles. Repeat several times during the day to relieve stress and tension. Your breathing pattern should be steady and smooth; breathe in through your nose and exhale through your mouth.

Tension and Worry

Tension and worry can age us considerably by straining our muscles, increasing wrinkles, disrupting our sleeping patterns, and compromising our energy resources and energy level. Behavioral habits can reduce tension and worry.

There is a major difference between worry and stress. The latter has more to do with things we can actually identify and control, whereas worry is the free-floating nebulous anxiety about something that may or may not happen. Decreasing worries will impede the aging process, but how do we do that? One technique that I recommend is to separate worries into two categories: things over which you have control and things over which you have no control. Simply identifying the inevitable, such as death and taxes, reduces your worry by at least half, maybe even more. There is a great deal of wisdom that comes with aging, and sorting out what is worth considering from that which we cannot change is an example. It allows us to move on in our life. There is something quite empowering when you take control of a situation. Focus your energy and time on improving the end results. Apply the 20/80 rule. Simply stated, decide to spend 20 percent of your time on the problem and 80 percent on the solution.

One thing that can be very helpful is to establish a planned worry time. Set aside maybe twenty minutes during the day and tell yourself that whatever kind of worries you have that pop into your head, you will only deal with them during this twenty-minute segment. This takes a little discipline but you can do it. When you come to the designated time, sit down and really focus. Write out a worry or concern that you have and for that twenty-minute period allow yourself to worry. Worry like you have never worried before. Just force yourself to think of every single concern that you might have. There is something in psychology called paradoxical intent and what that simply means is that you force yourself to worry, in this case, like a champion. And when you do that, the opposite effect will occur. You will have worried so much and have forced yourself so hard to worry properly that what you will find in the end is you won't be so worried.

I often suggest to patients that it may be helpful to develop a kind of mantra when it comes to worry. It's a self-soothing mechanism or technique that allows you to say something in lieu of the worry. For example, if you begin to worry, you say to yourself, "I'm feeling fine. I'm under control. I can handle things." Do that three or four times, until the worry passes.

It is said that "music soothes the savage beast" and is another effective tool in worry reduction. Research from the *Journal of the American Association of Nurse Anesthetists* found that the soothing sounds of Brahms concertos reduced the heart rate and blood pressure of individuals under anesthesia. Other studies have reported that soothing music reduces psychological anxiety. Classical music is commonly regarded as calming, as are tapes of the ocean, nature sounds, and babbling brooks. It is up to the individual to find the music that is harmonious to the soul.

When life presents you with a lemon, are you able to make lemonade? To go to the next level, are you able to not only make lemonade but to also share that abundance with others? If your answer to the latter is yes, then you are a member of a very unique and elite group of people called survivors. People who are able to experience a tragedy and not only prevail, but to actually excel are proven to live longer. Cancer patients who defy the odds and live in spite of their doctors' predictions seem to have some specific traits common to one another as well as to other types of survivors. Karl Simonten, M.D. found in his landmark studies with cancer survivors that these never-say-die patients were involved in their treatment and refused to give up. Their countenance was cheerful, they lived each day to the fullest and clearly celebrated life. Most had maintained close loving relationships and were able to garner strength from friends and family. Remarkably these special patients not only sustained their own strength, but provided it to others. Survivors seemed to have multiple interests and hobbies and were human doers not just human beings. Most possessed a profound sense of faith and felt nurtured by a loving God. They had reasons to live, and, while some had to say all-too-soon good-byes, they died not feeling defeated when their quest to live was not fully realized.

Whether you are an optimist or a pessimist, your attitude can increase or reduce tension. Much of our angst and worry is self-induced. At that juncture, slowing down and reprogramming our thinking is the next step. Perfection is not possible. Be happy with your best efforts. Keep in mind that much worry may be due in part to what you think others think and expect. Ease up on yourself and express your concerns clearly and calmly. You might be very surprised of what the true thoughts and expectations of others really are.

What I have found to be true and definitely worth repeating is that a lousy attitude may be the product of a habitual lousy thought process. If you feed yourself miserable, unhappy, and self-deprecating thoughts, how could you expect to be anything other than their totality? Conversely, loving, kind thoughts create an optimist. Your work may be cut out for you. Just remember that it is not possible to hold two contradictory thoughts at the same time. What this means to you is that you can choose which thoughts you hold. Is it more beneficial to think positively or negatively? You can decide for yourself.

Humor might be the best medicine for worry and tension. Having a sense of humor and an ability to laugh at yourself is extremely beneficial in coping with the aftermath of a challenging dilemma. Humor is a way to help us distance ourselves from problems and disappointments and also provides an avenue for seeing those problems from a realistic perspective.

Ask yourself: *In terms of the universe, just how important (or embarrassing) is this situation?* Most of the time, thank goodness, it truly is of little consequence. Laughing physiologically increases the release of endorphins in your brain, which positively affects your mood, and thus how you age. When you run the risk of making a wrinkle, it better be worth it.

Independence

Aging is an inevitable process, but does not have to be an unhealthy one. A well-balanced diet with appropriate supplements, exercise, and worry management techniques are all effective anti-aging tools. Changing our habits toward healthy endeavors can increase our life expectancy and also positively impact our quality of life.

Elderly patients, and then, not-so-elderly patients, have complained to me that they feel their adult children interfere too much. They value their children's interest in them, but they also value their own right to make decisions for themselves.

Sometimes as people grow older, adult children reverse the roles, acting more like a parent than a child. Everyone needs to feel autonomous, but sometimes well-meaning kids take things over, or at least try. Every person also needs to feel needed, and one of the ways in which this is achieved is to be able to hang on to the things you have. Elderly people begin to lose things. They lose some of their physical mobility and daily functions; they lose spouses and friends—many of the things that create and maintain one's identity. A feeling of helplessness, worthlessness, and a deep sense of being useless that may trigger depression can ensue.

The more years you live, the more it becomes somewhat inevitable that you may need more help as time goes on. But if your mind is fairly alert and your judgment is sound, there is no reason that your desires and decisions should not be honored. In an attempt to avoid hurt feelings, older people may give in and feel compromised, but resentful feelings can be dealt with rather easily and need not be a problem.

It's okay to talk to your children about your concerns in a kind but firm fashion, and we call this method "setting boundaries." Explain how you feel and voice what your needs are. Adult children are busy; they want to help, but they need your direction and input. Let them know that one "role" you wish to maintain as long as possible is that of a reasonably independent adult, and that means you take an active role in all decisions that involve your health, finances, and lifestyle. Compromises can be reached if everyone understands each other's needs and point of view. Additionally, you might want to remind them about that other very important role that you play—you are still their parent!

Behavioral Helpers

Suggestions for Aging Well

- Be proactive. Don't just sit around; think of things to do and do them.
- If your family is far away, make a new one from friends.
- Give faith a chance.
- Worry is misuse of imagination. Use it to create.
- Get involved in church or synagogue.
- Act like a hero—choose several heroes and let them inspire you. It's never too late.
- Accept a compliment with grace and then give one.
- Consider getting a part-time job.
- Say "no" to yourself—it developsdiscipline, which leads to self-respect. Do two things every day that you don't want to do.
- Join a group, make new friends, visit your neighbors.
- Serve others—be encouraging and supportive. Volunteer; read to a child.

- Place a meaningful phrase up on your mirror.
- Be grateful.
- Laugh.
- Make a list of people who love you.
- Think of things as *easy*.
- Make small goals—small wins increase motivation.
- Do not create your future from your past.
- Fear is a counselor, not a jailer.
- It's not what you *can* do in life—it's what you *do*.
- When you get frustrated, honor that feeling—it means that your brain is searching for an answer.
- Play games to maintain your brain power and to be with others.
- The power behind momentum is commitment.
- Face the sun—what you look at grows in your life.
- You are a masterpiece in progress. Yes, even now.
- Change is contagious.
- Look for blessings, always—they will be there.
- Simplify your life.
- Without a plan, you become bored and confused. This zaps your motivation.
- Instead of worrying, ask—What can I do about this?

- Learn a new skill—how abou[t the] computer?
- Be curious, ask questions.
- Forgive.
- Make an album of your life to [give to] your grandchildren.
- Talk to yourself—talking is the [highest form of] thinking.
- Being touched is important to g[ood health.] Hug others; get a massage.
- Get dressed every day—fix your [hair and] makeup.
- Learn what makes you happy and [do it.]
- Indulge yourself.
- Be creative—most people wait for [a crisis or] crises; they react, then create. Plan [ahead.]
- Dance.
- Fatigue comes from not finishing a p[roject.]
- Look in a mirror and smile gently a[t your] reflection.
- A great motivator is to see how far [you've] come and review your accomplishm[ents.]
- Turn a project into a game—it will [excite and] empower you.
- Relax by *doing* something.
- Welcome your problems—they *all* [have] solutions.
- Play tapes that are inspirational; [use] drive time to educate and motiva[te] yourself regardless of your age.

- Be a thinker, not a whiner.
- Express your thoughts with kindness.
- Come to your own rescue.
- Love yourself in order to love others.

Herbs for Your Nerves

◆ DHEA ◆

Hormone levels in our body are greatly affected by the aging process. Dehydroepiandrosterone (DHEA) is a natural hormone made by gonads and adrenal glands. DHEA supplements can help with sleep, memory, and our ability to handle stress. Perhaps the most exciting news about DHEA is that it may protect us against Alzheimer's disease. DHEA levels peak in our twenties and gradually decline. Taking 10 to 25 milligrams of DHEA daily may help our aging brain stay at an optimum level. DHEA is associated with estrogen and progesterone, as I mentioned in a previous chapter. Women taking estrogen supplements after menopause may be at a lower risk for Alzheimer's disease, because it stimulates the growth of their brain cells and impedes the stress-related release of cortisol. Pregnenolone, a DHEA building block, will increase cognitive functions such as memory and concentration. The hormone is closely associated with our moods and vitality.

Interestingly, DHEA does not appear to have any specific function, so it is believed to have a role in supplying the body with what it needs in order to maintain appropriate levels of hormones. DHEA blood levels begin to decline around the second decade of life. The ability to balance hormonal levels may prevent age-related degeneration disorders. People who take DHEA enthusiastically embrace its rejuvenating qualities. DHEA appears to be a safe supplement when taken daily (10 to 25 milligrams per day). There are some mild side effects such as acne and facial hair, but they diminish quickly when DHEA is stopped.

◄ HGH ►

One of the most exciting areas of anti-aging is the research that is ongoing regarding human growth hormone, otherwise known as HGH. Once the province of the young, today HGH is considered by many to be the fountain of youth. HGH can rejuvenate a beleaguered immune system, help you lose weight, gain muscle, grow hair, erase wrinkles, increase sexual performance, and empower the brain. Longevity is here. Look young, and of equal importance, feel young.

This miracle comes with a price. First of all, you can only obtain HGH from a physician. It must regularly be injected and is extremely expensive. For some, it is worth the cost and inconvenience. There are some liquid synthetic forms of HGH but their efficacy is questionable. Many of the pharmaceutical houses are now engaged in serious clinical trials with promising results. Research and development is trying to keep up with the baby boomers' demand to recapture youth.

Seaweed

While diving into the ocean to find a source of vitamins and minerals may not be on a daily agenda, recent findings regarding the medicinal purposes of seaweed may warrant another look at it.

Seaweed is thought to help reduce the rate of breast cancer, obesity, and arthritis. It may also help lower blood pressure and help lessen the effects of infectious diseases. Chlorella is the botanical name for fresh water green algae. It contains all of the essential amino acids, nucleic acids, fibers, vitamins, and minerals, as well as many other nutrients.

Chlorella has a long list of health benefits, including: enhancing the immune system; increasing the number of beneficial flora in the gastrointestinal tract, which helps in treating ulcers, colitis, Crohn's disease, and diverticulosis; and promoting better digestion.

Seaweed is beneficial to the sensory nerves and membranes around the brain, spinal cord, and brain tissue. It is also beneficial for thyroid functions, constipation, and gastrointestinal upsets.

Royal Jelly

Royal jelly (previously cited) derives its name because it is the substance that makes a queen bee a queen. Immature worker bees secrete royal jelly and this jelly makes ordinary bee larvae into queen bees. It is said that the queen lives fifty times longer than an ordinary bee, is quite fertile, and has a higher level of stamina than worker bees.

Athletes who use royal jelly claim that they have increased stamina and a higher feeling of general well-being. Others claim that royal jelly increases the appetite, tones and strengthens skin, relieves weak and tired eyes, and rejuvenates the old. The jelly, according to some, is said to expand a human's lifespan and, in general, reinvigorate the body.

To use, take royal jelly in capsule form, 250 milligrams daily. It has no known side effects.

◄ Melatonin ►

Melatonin is a popular hormone used in replacement therapy. Typically known to help with sleep troubles, melatonin is actually an antioxidant that protects the brain from harmful free radicals. Taking 1 to 3 milligrams of melatonin close to bedtime will improve sleep patterns and perhaps slow brain deterioration. Investigators evaluating melatonin postulate that it may help deter the damage of Alzheimer's disease. It also shows some promise in fighting jet lag. Supplementation of melatonin is important as this hormone's presence in our bodies decreases as we age. This drop in melatonin can cause phase-shift insomnia, which simply means that you fall asleep later than you wish, and the result is you feel very tired and fatigued the next day. Phase-shift insomnia can become chronic. Melatonin can help you get back on track.

A word of caution: Melatonin should be taken

one hour prior to sleep. It works in concert with "the sun going down," and, if you take it immediately before retiring, you may be groggy the next day. To use melatonin, begin with 1 milligram, which you may increase to 3 milligrams if needed.

◄ Choline ►

Choline is a nutrient essential to brain function. It is part of the vitamin B complex. It stimulates the brain to secrete acetylcholine, a neurotransmitter that is directly related to memory. It is contained naturally in egg yolks, meat, and fish. The downside is that those foods are very high in cholesterol. Another way to get choline is through lecithin, which can be found in soybeans. One hundred milligrams per day in a capsule is a great idea.

◄ Aromatherapy ►

Your brain depends on sensory information to function properly, so use your nose. To relax before going to sleep, use lemon-scented eucalyptus, but during the day when you want to be fresh and alert, niaouli, an evergreen from the Outback, invigorates and clears out your sinuses.

Chapter 11
Pain

Personality is born out of pain.
It is the fire shut up in the flint.
— J. B. Yeats

All of us experience some pain throughout the course of our lives. From a scrape on our knee after falling off of our bike and a sprained wrist after a game of touch football to carpal tunnel syndrome and battling cancer, we search day in and day out for ways to lessen the pain. But, what about the people who suffer from daily bouts with pain? According to the American Pain Society, 65 million

Americans suffer from painful illness each year. With pain come not only the physical problems associated with it, but when left untreated, pain can be the source of innumerable difficulties: familial problems, decreased productivity at work, or even unemployment.

Yet it is difficult to label pain as a negative. Pain is complex. A stabbing pain alerts us to injury, but a daily, chronic pain serves no useful purpose. And while medications and other therapies may provide relief for one syndrome, they may not be effective in dealing with another type of pain. Each situation calls for a specific treatment that sometimes makes pain management a guessing game.

This chapter will not focus on the occasional pain associated with a fall or a broken bone. Instead, the focus will be on the chronic pain associated with fibromyalgia, headaches, and arthritis and the possible remedial properties of magnets, acupressure, acupuncture, and other alternative techniques.

Fibromyalgia

Fibromyalgia mainly affects muscles and their attachments to bones, especially in the area of muscle–tendon junctions. Fibromyalgia is a chronic pain and causes stiffness and aching at specific points of the body. It is one of the most common rheumatic complaints in North America. The pain and stiffness may occur throughout the entire body or may be restricted to certain locations as in myofascial pain syndrome.

Causes and Symptoms

While causes of fibromyalgia are not known, doctors have assigned a variety of factors that *possibly* contribute to its onset:

- A traumatic emotional experience
- Stress and/or depression
- Deficiencies in minerals (magnesium, oxygen, phosphate)
- Chronic fatigue
- Disruption of deep sleep

Fibromyalgia is a mystery that goes unsolved, with many of the causes for its onset still unknown. Doctors have categorized fibromyalgia as a syndrome, meaning that there are a set of signs and symptoms that occur together when a person suffers from it. Some of the symptoms include:

- Tenderness at eleven to eighteen specific sites
- Chronic aching, in specific areas, may be sharp
- Stiffness
- Muscle spasms
- Sleep disorders

- Fatigue
- Stress/anxiety
- Vitamin/mineral deficiencies
- Depression

Any of these symptoms alone may be cause for concern or to see a doctor. When they occur together, they signal a larger problem that should be treated as soon as possible.

Pain and stiffness are the most prominent symptoms of fibromyalgia and may develop gradually. The pain generally begins in one region and spreads throughout the body. Fibromyalgia throughout the body is more common in women than men. Men are more likely to develop myofascial pain or fibromyalgia in a particular location such as the shoulder or neck. Even though fibromyalgia is not life-threatening, the chronic persistence of the accompanying symptoms are very disruptive to a normal life. Fibromyalgia is but one of the many syndromes associated with chronic pain. If you believe you suffer from it, consult your doctor.

Sleep disorders and fatigue are associated with fibromyalgia as well. If a person suffers from it, lying in the same position for an extended period of time may cause pain. The fatigue associated with fibromyalgia is a "brain" fatigue in which the person is totally drained of energy. Stress and trauma are other symptoms. Severe stress coupled with emotional, traumatic experiences over a period of time and the body's negative reaction to this stress and trauma could trigger fibromyalgia.

Other symptoms that are not easily spotted but may be identified through laboratory studies include magnesium and manganese deficiencies. Magnesium helps the body boost energy production and manganese directly influences the metabolic rate.

Minerals and Vitamins

As of this moment, fibromyalgia is incurable, but there are many ways in which a person suffering from the syndrome can lessen the pain associated with it. Boosting the body's supply of certain vitamins and minerals by adding daily supplements to your diet can help. Magnesium can help in calming the body as it is known as the "antistress" mineral. Calcium supplements also produce a calming effect on the body, but more importantly it is the most abundant mineral found in the body and keeps bones healthy and strong. Other possible supplements include potassium, zinc, phosphate, and iron. Increasing your vitamin intake of vitamins A, C, E, B_1, B_2, B_3, B_6, and B_{12} may also assist in the treatment of fibromyalgia. As with adding any vitamin and mineral supplements to your daily regimen, consult your physician first.

While boosting the body's supply of certain vitamins and minerals may help the body in dealing with fibromyalgia, herbal supplements may be just as beneficial. Let me suggest several.

Herbs for Your Nerves—Fibromyalgia

◄ Red Clover ►

Red clover is a natural blood purifier and helps boost the immune system. When taken in its liquid form, it helps the body produce energy that may combat the fatigue associated with fibromyalgia. The recommended dose is 1,200 milligrams taken with food twice daily.

◄ Goldenseal ►

Goldenseal is a vinelike plant with little white flowery blossoms and that grows wild in North America. It is an herb that goes directly to the bloodstream and boosts a sluggish glandular system. It has been widely used by Native Americans to treat skin disease and to soothe sore eyes. Recent research confirms that the dried rhizome possesses cytotoxic activity, which explains its usefulness against viruses. Goldenseal contains alkaloids that produce a strong astringent effect on mucus membranes, which, in turn, reduces inflammation.

◄ Gotu Kola ►

Gotu kola increases circulation and balances hormones. Its main function in combating fibromyalgia is its ability to decrease the effects of mental fatigue and memory loss.

Gotu kola is a pretty plant with large, fan-shaped

leaves and grows in marshlike conditions. The big leaves contain asiaticoside, a soothing agent used to treat burns. It is available in capsule form or can be used as a tea or tincture. To make tea, use one or two dried gotu kola per cup of boiling water and drink it twice daily. **Caution:** Do not use if you are pregnant or nursing because some studies suggest that it may have a narcotic effect.

◄ Glucosamine Sulfate ►

Glucosamine sulfate is a key substance in determining how many water-holding molecules are formed in cartilage. Increasing levels of this supplement may alleviate the pain associated with arthritic conditions.

◄ Chondroitin Sulfate ►

Chondroitin sulfate is another supplement that can help treat pain associated with fibromyalgia. It inhibits the destruction of cartilage by certain enzymes. It helps promote cellular nourishment and lubricates the joints to allow better nutrient transport.

Headaches

Another source of chronic pain is headaches. Millions of Americans suffer from pain associated with headaches—tension-types, migraine, cluster, hormone, sinus, menopausal, or menstrual, to name a few. Unfortunately there seems to be no one treatment for all types of headaches, although treatments for each type are available.

Tension-Type Headaches

There are two classes of tension-type headaches—episodic and chronic. Episodic are the ones that probably everyone has experienced. It is a random headache often caused by stress, anger, or fatigue. Chronic are those headaches that occur daily for months at a time. Depression, physical problems, or psychological issues may explain their etiology. Other possible causes for these types of headaches include poor posture, bad lighting, or extended eyestrain. Over-the-counter medications that contain acetaminophen are often beneficial in relieving the pain of tension-type headaches. Relaxation techniques such as deep breathing or taking a brief walk may also decrease the pain.

Migraine Headaches

It is believed that 23 million Americans suffer from migraine headaches, and they occur more frequently in women than in men. Seventy percent of sufferers report that the headache occurs on one side of the head. A migraine generally begins as a dull ache and then develops into a constant, throbbing pain; the person may also experience sensitivity to light and nausea or vomiting. Headaches come in all sizes and intensity, so one specific cause of migraines is not likely; rather it is believed that they are triggered by stress, fatigue, caffeine, chocolate, or alcohol. Certain other types of food may also be responsible for triggering the headaches: canned or processed foods, onions, beans, avocados, peas, and so on. People who suffer from migraines might also find it helpful to reduce their salt intake and to avoid milk and ice cream. Tracking food intake is one of the best ways to determine possible triggers. Keeping a daily calendar of meals may be beneficial in pinpointing trigger foods. Counseling may also help, as some migraines are triggered by depression. Some over-the-counter medications have now been approved in treating migraines, and prescription-strength medications are also available. Ask your physician for a suggestion.

Cluster Headaches

Just as the name implies, cluster headaches are different from the two previously discussed because they come in groups. A cluster headache arrives with little or no warning and can last from thirty to forty-five minutes to several hours. The main difference between this type of headache and others is that it can reoccur, often a few hours after the first one. This pattern can continue for upwards of four successive headaches. Triggers of cluster headaches include smoking, drinking alcohol, and high levels of histamines in the body. While some over-the-counter medications may be useful in treating cluster headaches, it is important to note that some of the very ingredients contained in over-the-counter sinus or allergy medications may actually raise histamine levels in the body.

There are other types of headache as well. Some result from hormonal imbalances in the body—hormone headaches, menstrual headaches, and menopausal headaches. Others are associated with allergies or allergy medications—sinus and allergy headaches. *Be aware of the types of medications you are taking and their possible side effects.*

Chronic headaches are indeed maladies that cause millions of people pain. However, that pain can be treated or alleviated. Chronic pain associated with arthritis may not be as easily handled, as the next section will show.

Arthritis

Arthritis affects approximately 37 million Americans; that is, one in every seven Americans battles the pain associated with arthritis on a daily basis. Arthritis is a chronic pain that can last a lifetime. At the present time, there are more than 100 types of arthritis, ranging from tendonitis to bursitis to rheumatoid arthritis. Osteoarthritis or degenerative joint disease is the result of systematic loss of bone tissue in the joints and is the most common form of arthritis.

Most people associate arthritis with older people. Unfortunately, it can actually strike children and young people in the prime of their lives. There is no one specific cause of arthritis, but the best remedy is to properly diagnose it at an early stage. The major symptoms associated with arthritis are joint and musculoskeletal pain and inflammation of the affected area. Rheumatoid arthritis occurs in women more frequently than in men.

There seems to be a genetic predisposition to arthritis, and the misuse of anabolic steroids among some athletes may be another cause of the degenerative process. Arthritis gradually announces its onset by progressive pain and stiffness, but when you experience painful swelling and inflammation in the arms, legs, wrists, or fingers on both sides of the body, the diagnosis may be rheumatoid arthritis. Along with fatigue and sleeplessness, rheumatoid arthritis may cause damage to other parts of the body such as the heart, lungs, eyes, and nerves. It is most often the cause of the gnarled appearance of hands and feet in the elderly.

Arthritis is capricious. There are no known cures, and the disease may actually improve over time. Medications may help sufferers cope with the pain, improve joint function, and allow enjoyment of daily activities. One of the best ways to deal with arthritis pain is through regular, low-impact exercise designed to improve body functions and strengthen bones and joints.

Moderate exercise helps lessen the pain, increases the range of movement, and reduces fatigue associated with arthritis. Losing weight may also be a key factor in treating arthritis. Because additional weight on the body antagonizes the joints, losing that weight lessens the stress put on the knees, legs, hips, and other critical points of pain. Hydrotherapy, otherwise known as taking a hot bath, soothes the body and alleviates muscle tension. Though a bit radical, when all else fails, other treatment strategies include surgery or physical relocation to a hot, arid climate.

Ongoing research and clinical studies are changing for the better the way people cope with arthritis pain. The same is true for myriad other problems. As the world becomes a "global village," Eastern medicine and Western traditional medicine are intermingling and providing millions of people with alternative cures for the aches and pains that ail them, including the following.

Magnets

Recent attention has been paid to the possible remedial properties of magnets. African, Greek, Arab, Egyptian, Hebrew, and Chinese people have used magnets for remedial purposes for centuries, and now Western medicine is in the process of evaluating the efficacy of using them in treating aches and pains.

Magnets may ease the pain associated with tennis elbow, sprained wrists, broken bones, and other types of chronic pain. They are currently sold in wristbands, elbow braces, knee braces, ankle bands, and a variety of other bands and braces.

By wearing the band or brace with the magnet in it, the electrical fields of the body are believed to be changed. The change in the electrical fields is thought to be the key in the curative process of aches and pains. Magnets offer a safe alternative and there is indeed some research that supports the claims of users. At the current time, the use of magnets is neither approved nor disapproved by the FDA.

Hydrotherapy

A very old, tried-and-true form of relief can be realized in hydrotherapy—or therapy involving water in the form of ice, steam, or liquid. It has been used in psychiatry to calm agitated patients by placing them in large hot tubs, covered by blankets to keep the water warm and the patient calm. I have always lived near water and just watching it can be a very tranquil experience. It is believed that hydrotherapy was introduced in some forms by the Germans, who had a long fascination for spas and natural springs.

Today, hydrotherapy is a vital healing element used by physical therapists to treat burn victims, athletic injuries, chronic pain, stroke victims, circulatory problems, and bone and joint disorders. There are many other applications of hydrotherapy, and, of course, it is also a very big business. Hot springs spas have sprung up all over the world, and people pay a great deal of money to be pampered, massaged, and relieved of pain and stress.

If you live near the ocean or a lake or have a pool or hot tub in your back yard, you probably already know the relief one can achieve from just soaking in water. But if all you have is a bathtub, you are still in business. Create your own spa by incorporating some candles by the tub, some soft music, and, of course, some aromatherapy. Soaking in a hot bubble bath, preferably with a glass of wine, can relieve joint and muscle pain, calm your nerves, and prepare you for a good night's rest. You can convert your tub into a whirlpool by adding some inexpensive attachable jets.

Now, a real hydrotherapist would suggest that perhaps you alternate a hot bath with a cold shower to stimulate blood flow. They might also suggest that you toss in some oatmeal for your skin and perhaps some chamomile, but they probably would not let you have the wine.

Acupressure and Acupuncture

Other traditional Eastern forms of curing aches and pains are acupressure and acupuncture. Both acupressure and acupuncture have been used for thousands of years by the Chinese to relieve pain, correct body imbalances, and prevent illnesses. The key to acupressure is in pressure points found all over the body. By pressing on these points, blockages in the body's energy flow are opened and begin to heal. Acupressure uses rubbing, kneading, percussion, and vibration of the pressure points by human hands.

Acupuncture is built on the same foundation but differs from acupressure in its use of needles. There are generally six types of disposable needles used in acupuncture that vary in length, width of shaft, and shape of the head. They are inserted at certain parts of the body to stimulate the blocked channels.

However, Western medicine takes a more pragmatic approach to the benefits of acupressure and acupuncture. It is believed that the needles and pressure points when stimulated or pressed activate the nervous system to release endorphins and other hormones that affect mood, health, and pain.

There are no known side effects to acupressure or acupuncture. Both reduce tension, increase circulation, relieve stress, strengthen the immune system, and promote overall wellness.

Both acupressure and acupuncture are believed to be beneficial in the treatment of motion sickness, constipation, diarrhea, anxiety, depression, allergies, chronic fatigue syndrome, and pain associated with earaches, backaches, and knee pains.

Chiropractic Therapy

Misalignments of bones within joints, known as subluxations, are believed by chiropractors to cause an imbalance in the body that precludes the proper flow of nerve impulses and thereby creates disease. By using manipulation techniques that include quick hand thrusts or the use of a tool called an "activator," the chiropractor adjusts the joint and achieves alignment. Misalignment of bones and joints can cause muscle spasms, pain, deformity, and compromise your range of motion. Chiropractors do not use drugs; rather, they rely on physical therapy techniques that include a whole host of treatments from ultrasound to electrical muscle stimulation, massage, nutrition, and homeopathic remedies. Chiropractors are valued adjuncts in sports medicine and rehabilitation, and they often work in concert with an orthopedist, neurologist, or neurosurgeon.

A well-trained chiropractic physician can keep you off the surgeon's table, or at least delay the trip. It is a conservative form of treatment, but sometimes you need more help. Most medical doctors (M.D.s) can recommend a good chiropractor, so if you are looking for a referral, always check with your family doctor for a suggestion. You select a chiropractor the same way that you do any doctor—you talk to satisfied customers.

Biofeedback

Biofeedback is a high-tech method that teaches a patient to help control pain by way of computers. Electrodes are placed on the body over a muscle; they pick up electrical signals through the sensors and convert them into sound or images. These images are then displayed on the computer. A therapist teaches the patient how to control the intensity through relaxation techniques. When you relax, your blood pressure drops, and you are consciously controlling body processes.

People who are in pain tend to tighten up their muscles, a reaction to the anticipation of discomfort. That reaction only increases the pain, worsening the problem. Pain becomes a vicious cycle—the more you feel it, the more you dread it; the more you dread it, the more tense and anxious you become; and so you further stress the situation. By breaking the cycle, which can be achieved with instruction and practice, the muscles relax and tension diminishes. The process involves anywhere from six to ten sessions lasting about forty-five minutes each. It is impractical to carry around a computer everywhere you go, so the goal is to help you recognize the early warning signals without the aid of images or sounds. By listening to your body, you can stop (or reduce) the pain in its tracks. Biofeedback is especially helpful in the management of headaches.

Many Americans suffer from daily pain associated

with headaches, fibromyalgia, arthritis, and other ailments. While for some, there is no known cure, it is important to research and evaluate all possible options when dealing with each unique situation.

Behavioral Helpers

Because 65 million Americans are victims of chronic pain, it is increasingly important for people to consult their physician when symptoms appear and be willing to change their eating, exercising, and overall health habits. When the pain is treated with appropriate measures, there are lasting effects on every aspect of life.

1. Pain is a signal that all is not well, so if you experience it, talk to your doctor. Early detection and treatment is important.
2. Maintain good posture, especially when you are in front of a computer for a period of time. Sit up straight.
3. Take care of your feet. Wear shoes that support you and fit well.
4. Do stretching exercises periodically during the day.
5. Take a hot shower to relieve muscle tension.
6. Good nutrition is important for your body and your mind.
7. Feed your mind good thoughts. Avoid violent movies or things that can bring you down.

8. Maintain a healthy weight. Excess body fat stresses joints and bones.
9. Take medications or herbs according to the directions given. They are not suggestions.
10. Get a weekly massage. It does wonders. People need to be touched.
11. Listen to relaxation tapes. They work. Music and humorous tapes and movies stimulate the production of endorphins—natural morphine.
12. If you experience chronic pain, seek a support group. You need the encouragement and the opportunity to discuss what you are going through with empathetic listeners.
13. Treat yourself the way you wish others would treat you—with respect and kindness.
14. Practice patience and gratitude. Read inspirational material.
15. Eliminate as much stress from your lifestyle as possible.
16. If you have a project that requires physical activity, break it up in steps over a period of time. Don't be a weekend athlete.
17. Avoid conflict; problem-solve instead.
18. There are many gadgets and living aides on the market to help open jars, do chores, and make life easier. Look into it.
19. If you feel that your doctor is not helping, change doctors. There are many pain clinics

and options that you can research. Do it wisely and with caution. Take control.
20. Be optimistic and expect the best.

Herbs for Your Nerves

◄ Cayenne ►

Cayenne, long known as a spice, also has medicinal properties. It is a vibrant, red vine and can be found growing in Central and South America, from where it was imported to Spain and other parts of Europe. Sometimes it appears to be yellow and can be mild or very hot. It has been used to treat dyspepsia and diarrhea. When gargled, it can help ease the pain of a sore throat.

More recently, cayenne has been used in the treatment of diabetic neuropathy. Henry Ford Hospital in Detroit, Michigan, tested cayenne on fifteen patients suffering this disorder. Their results established its efficacy. Cayenne should be used to help treat neuropathy, especially when burning pain is associated with it.

It is a good source of vitamin C and also contains some iron and vitamin A. This hot little pepper can cause one to perspire, which ultimately cools the body down. It is very decorative and can be seen in tasteful displays on walls or tables. When you bite into a pepper, especially the hot variety, it packs a wallop, wakes you up, and some describe a sense of well-being. It's love at first bite!

Cayenne contains capsaicin, the "hot" part of the fruit, which acts as an irritant when applied to the body. When applied to the surface of the skin, it causes increased blood flow to the area of application. When used in this matter, cayenne reduces inflammation in that area.

To use, add one-half to one teaspoon of the pepper to one cup of boiling water. Or, in capsule form, take 30 to 120 milligrams daily. **Caution:** Excessive use of cayenne may cause liver or kidney damage and gastrointestinal problems. A possible side effect is hypersensitivity.

◄ Aloe Vera ►

Wall carvings found in Egyptian temples depict the use of aloe as early as the fourth century. It was used as a traditional funeral gift for the pharaohs. This greenish plant grows wild in desert regions and resembles a cactus. The Egyptians also used it in treating infections, the skin, hair loss, and hemorrhoids.

Aloe protects from infection and promotes the healing of minor burns and wounds. Today, the most common use of the gel is in the treatment of minor burns. Aloe moisturizes the affected area, which prevents the area from drying and thus helps heal it.

More recently, aloe has been found to alleviate the pain associated with arthritis. It has an anti-inflammatory property that promotes circulation. You can purchase a plant from a nursery; in Texas, we just dig one up. To use, break off a branch and apply a little of the liquid directly on the skin. **Caution:** Two FDA panels found insufficient evidence to support the healing properties of aloe vera in treating minor burns. Aloe is not approved as an internal medication, but its application externally is not known to cause severe reactions.

◀ Ginger ▶

Ginger is well known as a seasoning, but in China, Japan, and India it has been an essential part of medicine. It has been used since the sixteenth century to treat gastrointestinal upsets, and in China it has been used as a pesticide. It may also be found growing wild in the Caribbean and West Africa.

Ginger has also been used in treating motion sickness, dyspepsia, and other forms of nausea, and has recently been found to help headaches. The anti-inflammatory properties of the plant may relieve pain caused by the constriction of blood vessels and rheumatic conditions. The root is used, either fresh or dry, and is a light yellowish-greenish color with an exotic aroma.

Use one ounce of the rhizome to one pint of water. Boil the water separately and then pour over the plant and steep for five to twenty minutes. Drink one to two cups daily. You can apply fresh or grated ginger to the lower abdomen to relieve cramps. **Caution:** Excessive amounts of ginger may cause central nervous system depression and arrhythmias. If you have gallstones, consult your physician before taking the spice. Ginger is also known to cause heartburn.

◄ Feverfew ►

This plant is reminiscent of a daisy, with little white petals surrounding a large yellow blossom. Feverfew grows freely or in gardens. Traditionally, Greek and early European herbalists used feverfew. The English used it in drinks and wore it around the wrist to protect against fever and chills. It has a strong, lasting odor and has been planted around homes to purify the air. It may also be used to treat insect bites. Some people who use feverfew for extended periods have reported experiencing a mild tranquilizing effect, above and beyond the benefits that are received from pain relief.

Feverfew had fallen into disuse until recently, when it was found to alleviate the pain associated with migraine headaches. Its use as a preventative tool against migraines began in 1978. A study of seventeen patients, in which eight took feverfew, experienced fewer migraines than those on a placebo. Feverfew inhibits the production of certain acids that cause migraine, but its value is further realized for the treatment of pain associated with arthritis and even to treat dizziness.

Many migraine sufferers will eat the fresh

leaves, both for prevention as well as relief. However, a better method would be to steep two to four leaves in near-boiling water and drink it as a tea. Capsule form is also available. The problem with actually chewing on the leaves, as many people do, is that the leaves may cause mouth sores. **Side effects:** Mild withdrawal symptoms may be experienced after taking feverfew for treatment. Pregnant or lactating women and children under age two should not use it.

People who suffer from migraines might also find it helpful to reduce their salt intake, and avoid milk and ice cream. It is believed that perhaps some migraines are caused by food allergies; keeping a food journal may help in determining which foods cause the headaches.

◄ White Willow ►

White willow is one of the many trees in the willow family. It was found in various parts of Central and Southern Europe and was later introduced to the United States. It grows along rivers and streams and is very large and rough to the touch, with light brown bark on the trunk and grayish bark on the branches.

Greek physicians, such as Hippocrates, used white willow bark to treat pain and reduce fevers. Once introduced in the United States, Native American tribes, including the Pomos and the Natchez, used the bark in treatment of chills and fever.

White willow bark has been used to treat ailments ranging from dyspepsia to dysentery. For centuries, the bark has been used in the treatment of fevers and for pain relief. The ingredient in the white willow that is responsible for its medicinal uses is salicylic acid, which closely resembles aspirin. If you are allergic to aspirin, don't use white willow. Also, because of the salicylic acid, do not give it to children as they may develop Reye's syndrome, a potentially fatal condition that may damage the heart and brain.

To use, soak one to three teaspoons of the bark in one cup cold water for two to five hours and then boil the concoction and drink one cup daily.

◄ Wintergreen ►

Wintergreen was once used to flavor candies and gum, but it also can be used as an herbal remedy. Various Native American tribes, including the Sioux and the Nez Percé, used wintergreen to treat arthritis pain and sore muscles. Later it was used to alleviate headaches and colds. Wintergreen has been used as a stimulant, diuretic, and to treat rheumatism. The sweet, aromatic scent and flowering top blossom was a favorite of Thoreau, keeping him company in his wooded retreat.

More recently, wintergreen has been used as a component of over-the-counter balms and ointments to help relieve arthritis pain and muscle pain. Used externally, wintergreen oil treats body aches and pains. Since 1999, wintergreen has enjoyed the recognition of being Maine's state herb.

To use, take one 250-milligram capsule three times daily. **Caution:** Wintergreen is safe in proper dosages. When wintergreen oil is applied externally, it may cause skin irritation. Taken internally, wintergreen oil is poisonous, except in small amounts.

◄ Yarrow ►

The use of yarrow dates back to the Trojan War when it was known as *herb militaris* because it stopped wound bleeding. Yarrow was once dedicated to the devil, known as the "Devil's Nettle," "Devil's Plaything," or "Bad Man's Plaything," and was used in spells.

Yarrow is a modest little plant with feathery leaves and a flat clusterlike blossom that can be white or pink. It possesses an anti-inflammatory agent that can bring soothing relief to arthritic joints but also helps with hemorrhoids, runny nose, and PMS pain. Even though it has been used to treat allergies, there have been some reports of people developing a rash when picking the plant—so wash your hands, please.

Chewing its leaves may cure toothaches. Yarrow has also been used to lower blood pressure and improve circulation. More recently, yarrow was discovered to be beneficial in treating burns.

To use, add half an ounce of leaves to one pint of water. Boil the water and then pour it over the leaves and steep for five to twenty minutes. Drink one to two cups daily in the morning and in the evening. Use externally as needed. **Caution:** Contact dermatitis is a possible side effect, although it is not toxic.

◄ Mullein ►

With a tall, thick stalk that comes to a point displaying yellow flowers, mullein is one of those multipurpose herbs. Before the introduction of cotton, it was used to form the wick in candles and thus for a time was known as the "candlewick plant." It was believed that only witches used mullein for their candlewicks—and, thus, yet another nickname, "hag's taper," was born.

In different parts of Europe and Asia, it was said that mullein had the power to drive away evil spirits. In the classics, it is said that Ulysses took mullein with him to protect against incantations. It was introduced to America by early European settlers and smoked by Native Americans to relieve respiratory problems.

Mullein has been used in the treatment of scrapes, scratches, and even rug burn. It is also known to soothe a sore throat and lungs. Recently, mullein has been found to alleviate spasms and can relieve stomach cramps and help control diarrhea. The leaves may be chewed and eaten (although it does not have a pleasant taste) or boiled in water. Use half a teaspoon of leaves steeped in one cup of boiling water and drink as a tea. **Caution:** Mullein does have a sedative-like effect on the lungs.

◄ Peppermint ►

Pain tends to wear you down, so a helpful dose of aromatherapy with peppermint can perk you up. Peppermint has the additional benefit of relieving neuralgia and muscle pain.

Chapter 12
Weight

I worry about scientists discovering that lettuce has been fattening all along. . . .

—*Erma Bombeck*

Everyone at times feels out of control with food consumption. At any given moment, 20 million people in the United States are on some sort of diet for weight loss. "You are what you eat" is a common maxim in the world of nutrition. This simple adage refers to the belief that the human body is governed in almost every way by the food that it consumes and utilizes.

People often talk about eating a "balanced" diet, but what does this mean? Usually, we choose to eat the food we like rather than the food that is nutritionally best for our health. Our diet is made up of a mixture of different foods, and this is how we obtain a supply of all the nutrients our bodies need. There is no precise prescription for the sort of food and the amounts we must eat in order to stay healthy. Each individual has different nutritional needs. The best approach is to eat a range of foods from all the major food groups every day. There is growing awareness among the general public as well as nutritionists, scientists, and doctors that eating a "healthy" diet, which contains an adequate amount of all the essential nutrients our bodies need to function effectively, can help promote and maintain good health, both physically and mentally, and prevent disease.

There are many reasons that we eat—to give our bodies the fuel that they need, to boost our energy, as part of socializing with others, or because we are genuinely hungry. When we eat to fill emotional "holes" or needs, such as eating to celebrate, to mask feelings, to decrease feelings of anger, fear, sadness, anxiety, or depression, we are treading on shaky ground.

After many years in private practice, I have developed a hypothesis concerning the problem of obesity. Whether you are ten pounds or a hundred pounds over your appropriate weight, I believe that it has more to do with the obstacles and problems in your life (unmet needs, difficult childhood, and tragedy) than any other factor. When people come to my office, it is rarely about their weight, although many will tell me that it is a concern. They come to see me about depression, anxiety, relationship issues, traumatic experiences, self-esteem, physical, sexual, or psychological abuse, or problems with alcohol or drug abuse. An intricate aspect of their coping mechanisms is often related to overeating, the basis of which is really "what is eating them." Loneliness and a trend toward working at home can lend itself to feelings of depersonalization and often results in isolation. Snacks are always available; satisfying relationships may not be. Overweight people literally build a wall around themselves to keep safe or to keep others out.

This is not to say that all of us who tend to vary in our weight ten to twenty pounds are experiencing deep psychological problems. But, it might be fair to point out that those extra pounds didn't just get there by accident. Comfort food is more than just a description of what we like to eat.

When we begin to use food as a way to get through life's ups and downs, we are essentially self-medicating, much the way an alcoholic does with alcohol. And, as with alcohol, the "fix" is temporary. In addition, there is a rebound effect: In order to soothe the feelings of guilt, depression, shame, anxiety, and anger that come with the realization of our inappropriate behavior, we need more of the "medication" (food). Lastly, eating to deaden feelings solves nothing. No one can escape from their emotions, nor can you medicate them away.

Anyone who has ever tried to lose weight knows quite well there are a variety of diet-oriented products from which to choose. Some are very helpful—for example, health clubs and exercise programs. Of equal importance are the contributions that professional nutritionists, through their research, have made, which has increased our awareness of the impact proper food has on our overall health. Hypotheses on metabolism, insulin regulation, willpower, the merits of one diet over another, and, finally, the litany of articles on behavioral methods surely would have solved the problem by now. Many people ask questions regarding weight loss: "Is my metabolism too slow?" or "What can I take to curb my sweet tooth?" or even "Why was I cursed with my genetics?" These are good questions asked and reasked to no avail. My suggestion is to consider this: Maybe you have been asking the WRONG questions. Diets are all about what you eat. But the real question that desperately needs to be asked is: What is eating you? When you ask yourself that question, suddenly you have focused on the cause and not the symptom. When you ignore your emotions, you end up dealing with what the emotions look like.

So, ask yourself:

1. Why am I so unhappy?
2. Why do I feel so empty, confused, alone?
3. Why is it that no matter how hard I try, I cannot seem to lose weight and then keep it off?
4. How many more diet plans and programs will I have to try?

I am absolutely certain that if people could really understand what they are doing and why they do it, their preoccupation with unwanted weight would stop. They would be able to trade unhealthy eating patterns for more effective soothing skills.

Foods and Moods

One factor to consider when choosing an eating plan is how foods affect your mood. I have already mentioned neurotransmitters and their roles in behavior. But mood and behavior are similar, and food can trigger the mechanisms that control mood depending on the food you eat. Low levels of serotonin can make you feel irritable, hungry, and stimulate cravings for carbohydrates. Lowered levels of dopamine can cause you to feel sluggish and unfocused. A large steak may hit the spot. The brain also puts out endorphins, which create a natural high and may act much like morphine. Endorphins may cause cravings for fatty foods and create anxiety, but they also are a natural pain reliever and keep you in a good mood. A better way to stimulate production of endorphins is through exercise. Protein and complex carbohydrates are natural "pick-me-uppers." I am giving you a very brief explanation of the connection between food and mood. In reality, it is a very complicated biological/genetic/environmental process. So now I will get more practical.

Foods that are known to uplift are proteins, such as lean beef, chicken without skin, fish, peanut butter, cottage cheese, yogurt, cheese, peas, beans, soy, soy milk, and tofu. Broiling fish and poultry is another way to enjoy these foods without all the added fat. Foods that are known to calm are carbohydrates such as whole grain breads and crackers, corn, pasta, potatoes, and rice, especially brown rice.

An easy way to remember how foods affect you is to think of how a high-protein, low-fat breakfast makes you feel; for example, two scrambled eggs, two pieces of bacon, and a cup of coffee. Close your eyes and envision eating this sort of breakfast—can you feel the energy? Now, imagine eating a heavy breakfast; for example, three large pancakes dripping with butter and syrup and a cup of coffee. How does this make you feel?

Fatty foods make us feel tired and sluggish; they are harder to digest so they sit in our stomachs making us feel uncomfortable, making our stomachs rumble, even making us feel nauseated. For those late afternoon doldrums, try eating protein rather than fat. Also, frozen vegetables contain almost as many nutrients as fresh vegetables. When you cannot buy fresh vegetables, buy the frozen kind. When using canned vegetables, be sure to drink the liquid as the nutrients are in there.

Diets

If you drop the "t" from diet, you get the word "die"—something to think about! Unless you only have five to ten pounds or so to lose for maintenance reasons, diets don't work. Initially, you lose weight on almost any plan, but research suggests that when you lose twenty-five or more pounds on a diet, you will probably regain the weight and then some. Dieting leaves people feeling deprived, alienated, and angry.

One can become overwhelmed and totally confused when seeking the truth about diets. Patients tell me all the time about the latest craze and fad that they are trying, but the truth is, diets are often like get-rich-quick schemes—it sounds great but probably doesn't work over the long haul. If a diet promises too much, then let the buyer beware. If it seems too good to be true, it probably is.

I am going to give you a cursory sketch of two different approaches to achieving weight loss. The first is a diet that I occasionally use to lose five to seven pounds; the other I have never tried but thought it was interesting. Years ago there was some research that linked your blood type to your personality type—not exactly "hard science." This is the new spin, but with some impressive data.

The Atkins Diet

The Atkins Diet is the result of Robert C. Atkins, M.D., who specialized in bariatrics (the treatment of overweight problems), seeking the ideal diet. The basis of the diet is the induction of "ketosis," which is the burning of stored fat for energy. Dr. Atkins' clinical observations led him to publish that such a diet also worked for a variety of other problems, particularly cardiovascular, arthritis, and a host of other chronic degenerative diseases. The diet was referred to as the "Atkins' Low Carbohydrate Diet." The following is an outline of food regulations on this diet:

- *Animal foods (meat, fish, fowl, shellfish)*—are all allowed unless sugar, MSG, corn syrup, cornstarch, flour, pickling, nitrites, or other preservatives are used in the preparation.
- *Fats and oils*—despite the furor over "high-fat diets," many fats, especially certain oils, are essential to good nutrition. Butter is preferred over margarine and mayonnaise is permitted. The fat that is part of the meat or fowl (that is eaten) is permitted. For salad dressings, use the desired oil plus vinegar or lemon juice and spices. Grated cheese,

chopped eggs, and bacon may all be added.
- *Cheese (hard, semisoft, aged, yellow)*—avoid "diet" cheeses, cheese spreads, or cheese foods. From three to sixteen ounces per day are allowed. Examples are Swiss, American, Cheddar, Brie, Camembert, Mozzarella, Chèvre, Ricotta, cottage, farmer, and pot, as well as tofu.
- *Eggs*—permitted without restriction.
- *Salad vegetables*—leafy greens, asparagus, broccoli, string or wax beans, cabbage, beet greens, squash, mushrooms, cucumbers, celery, radishes, peppers, and bean sprouts are allowed (from two to six cupfuls per day).
- *Sorbitol, honey, fructose, lactose, sucrose, maltose, and dextrose* are NOT allowed.
- *The best liquids are water and herbal teas.*

Although Dr. Atkins was criticized by many, he stands firm because of his thousands of clinical success stories. Recent findings document that his moderately high protein and fat diet is not bad advice, and his severe curtailment of sugars is beneficial to many.

Eat Right for Your Type

"What would you say if I told you that the secret to a healthy, vigorous, and disease-free living might be as simple as knowing your blood type?"

asks Dr. Peter D'Adamo, author of *Eat Right for Your Type*. In his book, he shows us the simple answer—our bodies assimilate food differently based upon blood types: A, B, AB, or O. His theory is that our metabolism speeds up with some foods and slows down with others and that our blood type can help us regulate a more appropriate diet. Dr. D'Adamo's father first discovered this concept over thirty years ago as he was treating patients with heart problems and patients with severe diabetes. He noticed that each blood type responded differently to his treatments and further noticed he could control the patients' problems depending on what they ate. His son Peter, the author of this book, spent the last fifteen years researching the connections among blood types, food, and disease.

- The blood type O is very old; it is the original blood type of the Earth, belonging to the "hunter-gatherers," and the diet consists of the same things today that our ancestors ate then: meat (high protein, low carbohydrates), no wheat or most other grains. The best form of exercise for this group is vigorous and aerobic.

  Risk factors for ulcers and inflammatory disease such as arthritis are high for this group if eating incorrectly for this type.
- The blood type A appeared on Earth between 22,500 and 15,000 B.C. in

response to new environmental conditions—the advent of agriculture. Type As are called agrarian. The diet that works best for people with this blood type is essentially vegetarian (high carbohydrates, low fat) and includes vegetables and soy products, and grains and cereals. It is best for this group to engage in gentle exercises such as yoga or golf and meditate to deal with stress.

Risk factors for cancer and heart disease increase for this group if eating incorrectly for this type.

- The blood type B evolved sometime between 15,000 and 10,000 B.C. and is a combination of A and O. This blood type emerged as a result of the migration of the races from the African homeland to Europe, Asia, and the Americas and may have mutated due to climactic changes. Type Bs are called balance—their diet is a combination (or balance) of As and Os: the most varied diet of all the types, including meat; it is the only type that does well with dairy products. Engaging in moderate forms of exercise such as swimming or walking is best for this group.

Risk factors for slow-growing viruses that attack the nervous system increase for this group if eating incorrectly for this type.

- The blood type AB emerged only in the last 1,000 years as a result of the intermingling of Caucasians with Type B Mongolians. Less than 5 percent of the world has this blood type.

  People with this blood type have the benefits and intolerances of both type As and type Bs.

  Engaging in exercises and relaxation techniques are best for this group. People with this blood type have the friendliest immune systems.

Behavioral Helpers

If you want to maintain or begin a healthy eating plan, then pay attention to your intake of cholesterol. The total intake of cholesterol should be less than 300 milligrams a day. One egg yolk contains 250 millligrams. Eating three eggs a week is plenty. Cutting back on red meat, poultry with the skin and fat still on, whole dairy products, palm and coconut oils (found in crackers), cookies, and nondairy creamers can help cut cholesterol significantly. Use unsaturated fat cooking oils such as corn, olive, canola, safflower, sesame, soybean, and sunflower. Steer clear of fried foods.

If you still want that quick weight loss fix to help boost self-esteem and feel better about yourself again, then metabolism plays a key role in this. Many people believe that starving themselves is the key to weight loss. Actually, our bodies go into starvation mode when they are deprived of the food, and hence nutrients, that they need to function efficiently and properly. Many prominent dieticians claim that if people wake up their sleeping metabolisms, we'd all weigh 10 to 15 percent less than we do now. To wake up your sleepy metabolism, try the following behavioral helpers.

- Use the morning sun as a trigger—there is mounting evidence that exercising in natural morning light gets our metabolisms working faster and sooner. Just about any morning activity will give you a head start—playing with the dog, yard work, even a short walk to work.
- Balance your carbohydrates—studies have shown that carbohydrates tend to trigger a flood of the hormone insulin, a flood that makes cells seal themselves up so they won't drown in the stuff. And when cells seal up, the food we eat can't descend into them to be burned as energy—so it winds up as fat instead. One researcher had her patients switch to fewer carbohydrates at the same time allowing them all the protein, fat, and nonstarchy vegetables they wanted. The results are the people who thrive on this kind of eating plan naturally find their own balanced way of eating.

- Eat more—many of us try too hard to diet, and we actually eat too few calories in the process. As a result, our metabolism is sluggish as it is not being fueled efficiently enough to keep the body's engine stoked. Also, constant skimping means our metabolism isn't getting all the nutrients it needs, such as fiber and protein, to operate at peak proficiency.
- Eat more often—eating actually stimulates the metabolism. In fact, you burn calories 10 to 25 percent faster for about an hour after each meal.
- Drink green tea—a breakthrough University of Geneva study has found that green tea accelerates your metabolism. Test subjects who took 150 milligrams daily doses of caffeinated green tea extract began burning calories 4 percent faster than before. Researchers reason that a natural chemical in the tea reacts with the caffeine, incinerating extra calories in the process. Unlike many diet pills, the green tea showed no signs of increasing heart rate.
- Tone your abdominal muscles—in a study by a YMCA fitness pro, test subjects who combined muscle-toning exercises with aerobics lost twice as much fat as those who did aerobics alone.
- Discover and use sports supplements carefully—whether in capsule or powder form,

creatine had been proven to increase energy production in our cells and increase the speed at which we build calorie-hungry muscle. Use caution, however. Discuss creatine with your doctor before using.

Physical Activity Tips

Experts agree that you must move in order to lose weight and keep it off. Here are some helpful hints:

- Cross-training (that is, combining aerobic activities such as stationary bike, skipping rope, or jogging) with intermittent muscle toning (working out with Nautilus equipment, free weights, or calisthenics) is the most effective method.
- Daily walks along with some muscle toning is also effective.
- Workouts should last about forty-five minutes, five times per week.
- Physical activity increases stamina, energy, and overall feelings of wellness.
- Physical activity greatly enhances emotional well-being, improves your attitude, increases concentration and focus, and decreases depression and anxiety.
- To maintain your ideal weight after weight loss, you need to exercise three times each week.
- A five-minute warm-up followed by a sustained, intense, twenty-minute workout should

be followed by a ten-minute cooldown.
- Physical activity increases your metabolic rate and leads to increased weight loss in less time than achieved with diet alone.
- Physical activity preferentially burns fat instead of muscle.
- Physical activity lowers your risk for heart disease.
- Physical activity tends to *reduce* your appetite and prevents constipation.
- If you have not enjoyed physical activity for a long period of time, begin slowly and gradually build.
- To relieve muscle soreness that may accompany a new routine, stretch first, soak in a hot bath afterwards, and use an anti-inflammatory agent for discomfort.
- Any type of activity from housework to dancing burns calories.
- It is wise to vary your exercise routine so you will not get bored and are thus more likely to continue.
- Finding a "buddy" helps with "stick-to-itiveness."
- Tell friends you are exercising. You will be putting a little pride on the line.
- If you do not enjoy your current routine, change it.
- Once again, you need a plan that includes a specific designated time and place.

Weight Loss Tips

- Weigh yourself only one time per week.
- Keep a small note pad handy to keep track of what you eat, recording the type of food, the amount, and the time of day you eat it.
- Buy a small food scale and start weighing what you are eating. Are your serving sizes too large?
- Establish a reward system that encourages your success. Make a list of nonfood treats.
- When you recognize a "trigger," use positive self-talk instead of eating.
- Use your good china, eat at the table, and use candles. Make it special.
- Don't eat in the car, at your desk, while shopping, while walking, while watching TV, while talking on the phone, at the movies, or while cooking.
- Use smaller plates.
- Don't rush through meals.
- Plan all meals ahead of time when you are NOT hungry.
- Make grocery lists and shop only when you are NOT hungry.
- Prepare some meals ahead of time and freeze them. If you are in a hurry, you can defrost the meal instead of grabbing for junk food.
- Don't eat food you don't want just to be social or polite, or when you are bored.

- When eating out, plan ahead what you will order.
- Make special requests in restaurants; e.g., dressing on side, broiled not fried, etc.
- Be a label reader.
- Look for low-calorie or low-fat alternatives.
- Experiment with herbs and spices.
- Reduce your salt intake.
- Include vegetables and fruit at each meal.
- You must eat to lose weight.
- Eliminate alcohol from your food plan until you reach the maintenance stage.
- Drink six to eight glasses of water daily.

Herbs for Your Nerves

◄ HCA ►

HCA is a supplement extracted from the rind of a Southeast Asian tamarind. In studies over many years, HCA has been shown to enhance energy production. HCA actually limits the body's production of a chemical required to convert the food we eat to stored fat, forcing it to burn more of the food we eat and burn it more quickly. Therefore, more calories become energy and fewer are stored as fat. Also, HCA has been shown to reduce appetite.

◄ Ephedra ►

Ephedra, also known as ma huang, has been used by the Chinese for over 5,000 years to treat asthma and upper respiratory problems. It is also a known stimulant similar to caffeine.

Recently, ephedra and its main constituent, ephedrine, have been touted to increase metabolic rate and reduce calorie consumption. In this manner it has been used to help in weight loss and to suppress the appetite.

To use, boil one pint of water and pour over half an ounce of ephedra and steep for five to twenty minutes. Drink one cup daily in the morning. **Caution:** There is no reliable evidence that ephedrine is safe or effective in weight loss. Ephedrine raises blood pressure and can lead to stroke. *It has been linked to the deaths of at least fifteen people.* Discuss it with your doctor before using.

◄ Schizandra ►

Schizandra is found in China, Japan, and Korea where it has been used for centuries. In China, schizandra is one of the most important herbs. It has been used to help lower stress and increase the energy supply of cells in the brain, liver, muscles, and kidneys. It has also been used to preserve beauty and as a seditive.

Recently, the focus on schizandra has shifted to its powers as an appetite suppressant; it may be beneficial to those trying to lose weight, it improves the digestion of fatty foods, and increases the production of bile.

To use, take one tablet or capsule daily. **Caution:** Schizandra should not be used during pregnancy or by people who have high blood pressure, peptic ulcers, or epilepsy.

◄ Chitin ►

Chitin is a natural product, a polysaccharide found in the exoskeleton of shellfish. It is a fat blocker that "sponges" up fat in the digestive tract. Possibly, you have seen the impressive advertisements on TV where they demonstrate chitin's effectiveness by placing a lump of fat in water containing chitin, and, miraculously, it is absorbed on contact. Chitin is used in water treatment facilities as it attracts grease, oils, and other potentially hazardous waste material. In the body it does the same thing.

Many claims have been made about chitin's remarkable abilities. It appears to be safe, but perhaps should be used for short intervals to lose weight and keep it off. There are no short cuts to a proper diet and exercise. One problem associated with this substance is that it may indiscriminately absorb vitamins and minerals in the process, so you need to take your vitamins before you go to bed.

In order to maximize its potential, chitin should be taken thirty to forty-five minutes prior to a meal.

Multivitamins and Mineral Supplements

Everyone who is trying to lose weight needs to

assist the body in maintaining enough vitamins and minerals to keep you going. At the minimum, a daily multivitamin is absolutely necessary and cannot be overemphasized. Depending on the type of diet that you have chosen—for example, a high-protein diet or a low-fat diet—you will need to adjust your dietary supplements accordingly.

Chapter 13
Eating Disorders

Even though half of the American population is overweight, obesity is not usually listed as an eating disorder. The two most common eating disorders are anorexia nervosa and bulimia nervosa. Persons suffering from anorexia are typically adolescent women with low self-esteem, depression, and the feeling that they are out of control. Anorexia can be defined as self-starvation due to excessive dieting.

Bulimia is a form of eating disorder characterized by eating large quantities of food followed by purging the food through laxatives or vomiting. Like anorexia, bulimia is more commonly found in young women with poor self-esteem and feelings of powerlessness.

Although no one cause has been singled out for either disorder, researchers believe it may be a combination of factors: family and cultural demands, chemical imbalances, emotional and personality disorders, and even genetics.

Family pressure may greatly impact the likelihood of developing anorexia or bulimia. Research cites that mothers often encourage their preteen daughters to lose weight. It appears that mothers of anorexics are often overly preoccupied with the life of their child. Mothers of bulimics are typically found to be critical and uninvolved in the life of their child. Other family members may influence the eating habits of adolescent women; studies find that anorexics are affected by critical fathers and brothers. Bulimics and anorexics have been found to have increased incidences of sexual abuse. Furthermore, persons with eating disorders are more likely to have an alcoholic or drug-dependent parent.

More specific to persons suffering from bulimia, the fear of obesity may be a result of having an overweight parent. Compared to other psychological disorders, childhood obesity or parental obesity is found in greater rates in bulimic patients. Research has cited that bulimics more commonly report having dysfunctional families and experiencing emotional difficulty.

Genetically, studies are linking eating disorders with family history. There is evidence that anorexic patients experienced low birth weight, infections, seizures, physical traumas, and stomach and intestinal difficulties in infancy. Although a decisive genetic link has not been found, persons with anorexia are eight times more likely to have a relative with the malady. Other disorders associated with bulimia and anorexia have genetic links such as depression and obsessive compulsive disorder. Furthermore, studies are attempting to find connections between eating disorders and the genetics of neurotransmitters in the brain.

As with family influence, the media and culture impact the image we have of ourselves. Advertisements focus on weight loss and athletic bodies. Fashion magazines display anorexic models as the ideals. Clothes are designed and modeled for thin bodies, while fast food and junk food ads are rampant. Thus, the struggle to stay thin becomes a challenge.

Women with eating disorders begin to take pride in their ability to maintain an excessively low weight in spite of the food that surrounds them. Again, media reinforces the weight loss. Women may also find themselves the envy of their friends. As a result, a false sense of control and power is often developed in women with eating disorders. Women in competitive athletics often suffer from anorexia, which affects their menstrual cycle and postpones puberty. Female athletes may starve themselves to maintain a low body weight and impede the fatty tissues associated with breast and hip development. These women are influenced by the media's concept of an athlete and by the control of their coaches.

Chemical imbalances may also play a role in the development of an eating disorder. As with the emotional disorders commonly associated with anorexia and bulimia, researchers are not quite sure which comes first, chemical dysfunctions or the eating disorder. However, it is clear that persons suffering from anorexia exhibit abnormalities in their hormonal and neurological systems. The problem has been identified in the hypothalamus, a small area of the brain responsible for controlling the pituitary gland. Our hormonal and nervous system is regulated by the pituitary gland. Research indicates that anorexic patients release high amounts of the protein corticotropin in their brains during stressful events. The corticotropin-releasing factors act as appetite suppressants by blocking neuropeptide Y, an appetite stimulant. However, differing studies have indicated that the irregular amounts of the appetite-related chemicals have been found before and after the onset of anorexia. The question of whether hypothalamic-pituitary abnormalities are the cause or the result of anorexia remains to be answered.

Many scientists believe that a body's reaction to starvation may have an inherent link. These scientists have postulated that anorexic patients have an exceptional amount of natural narcotics that their brain releases during starvation, which encourages an addiction to a state of starvation. The scientists believe that the natural narcotics are hereditary in the families of anorexics. This may explain the increased likelihood of developing anorexia if a relative suffers from the eating disorder.

For bulimic patients, studies have focused on animals and war prisoners. It appears that persistent restriction of food may increase the tendency for bingeing that continues even after food supplies are regularly available. The act of vomiting or taking laxatives may provoke the manufacturing of natural opioids. Researchers hypothesize that the natural opioids act as narcotics in the brain, motivating the addiction to bulimia.

Finally, research has found a correlation between emotional disorders and patients with anorexia or bulimia. Some studies have reported as many as 96 percent of all patients with eating disorders also suffer from an emotional malady. Depression found in many anorexic patients begins to improve with weight gain. Persons with severe cases of anorexia and bulimia exhibit unusual levels of neurotransmitters in the brain, specifically serotonin. Serotonin levels in the brain directly impact depression and obsessive compulsive disorders.

As with depression, anorexia and bulimia are affected by seasons of the year. Darker, colder winter months mean more severity in depression. Bingeing and purging appears to increase in a subgroup of bulimic patients during the winter months, while anorexic onset is more prevalent in May, which is the month with the highest rates of suicide.

Anxiety disturbances such as obsessive compulsive disorders and panic disorders are typical in anorexia and bulimia sufferers. Studies indicate that obsessive compulsive disorders, characterized by persistent thoughts and rituals, precedes anorexia. Persons with anorexia become obsessed with counting calories, diet, exercise, and food. Rituals are often exhibited in constantly weighing themselves or cutting food into very small pieces. Panic disorders tend to follow the onset of anorexia, exhibited by the fear of public humiliation. Bulimics also report having similar social phobias. The anxiety disorders have been found to be improved by the progress of the anorexic or bulimic patient.

As with the variety of factors that may lead to the development of anorexia or bulimia, a variety of treatment options are available. Some have been found to be more effective than others, but most experts agree that combining different treatment approaches is most effective.

The first hurdle in treating persons with eating disorders is to help the patient recognize that medical care is needed. Breaking the cycle of purging and challenging the belief of emaciation as healthy and attractive is difficult. Specialists treating patients with eating disorders must set realistic expectations and goals. Patients and family members must understand that treatment will be difficult and painful. Relapse is common and should be accepted as part of the treatment process.

Beginning treatment for eating disorders focuses on weight gain. Persons with moderate to severe cases of anorexia or bulimia should be admitted to the hospital. A two- to three-month stay in a hospital or treatment center is optimal, but two weeks is more common. Once released from the hospital, persons with eating disorders begin outpatient therapy. Patients are typically encouraged to gain one or two pounds a week. The weight gain expectation is a non-negotiable aspect of treatment. Severely malnourished patients may experience stomach discomfort, bloating, fluid retention, and even heart failure. Thus, strict adherence to the calorie intake prescribed is essential. Patients are required to eat meals without discussing the disorder; meals should be eaten in a relaxed, supportive atmosphere. Intravenous feeding should only be used in extremely severe cases.

Because excessive and ritualistic exercising is often an aspect of an eating disorder, exercise in the treatment phase should be permitted with caution. Specific exercises may be encouraged for reducing stomach and intestinal discomforts. Exercises may be presented to the patient as reward and used in conjunction with appropriate eating habits. However, all exercise regimes must be monitored and carefully controlled.

Treatment for bulimia and anorexia requires the expertise of many specialists. Medical doctors, nurses, dietitians, psychologists, behavioral therapists, teachers, family members, and the patient must be actively involved in the treatment process. Studies indicate that the multidisciplinary team approach increases the likelihood of success.

Because weight gain is the goal for treating persons with eating disorders, it is necessary that medical doctors and dietitians work closely together to increase healthy calorie intake. As many patients are fragile from malnourishment, careful selection of food to provide optimum health and weight gain and minimize stomach and intestinal distress is necessary. Furthermore, patients need to be taught the risk factors associated with bingeing, purging, and self-starvation. Strategies for creating healthy meals and understanding good nutritional habits should be established.

Individual counseling with a psychologist is another step in the treatment process. Therapy addresses depression and anxiety commonly associated with the eating disorders. Patients learn to express their feelings and fears in an appropriate manner. Psychologists help the patients develop strategies for coping with change and doubt. Patients also explore past incidences of sexual abuse, neglect, or any traumatic events that may have negatively impacted their lives.

Behavioral Helpers

Common signs may telegraph an eating disorder. Persons suffering from anorexia and bulimia begin to exhibit changes that may notify loved ones of their illness. Wearing baggy clothing, though a current trend, may be the first indicator of a potential eating problem. Weight loss, preoccupation with counting calories, and excessive exercising are signals too. Physiologically, a person suffering from bulimia or anorexia may become constipated, lose hair, stop having a menstrual cycle, and exhibit little sexual desire. Behaviorally, bulimics often go to the bathroom right after a meal, insisting on being alone. Anorexics and bulimics may become obsessed with the fear of being fat, even if they are very thin. Dry, sallow skin and cold hands and feet may also be indicators of an eating disorder.

Behavioral therapists work with anorexic and bulimic patients by changing the inaccurate perceptions, thinking patterns, and beliefs about their own bodies. By changing this process, the patient's response to food begins to change to become more appropriate and typical. A behavioral component to this approach is essential. The patients are required to monitor and keep a log of their food intake, bingeing, purging, and any ritualistic behaviors associated with their eating disorder. The patient is forced to address habitual dysfunctions in their eating pattern and discuss it with their behavioral therapists. The goal is to help the patient recognize and challenge inaccurate ideals in body image, ideas about perfection, and the impacts of unhealthy eating. Patients are encouraged to replace their unrealistic beliefs with new healthy, accurate, and reasonable expectations.

Family therapy has been found to be particularly effective in very young patients because the family has a great amount of influence in this stage of their lives. As family dysfunction has been found to be prevalent in the lives of persons with anorexia and bulimia, addressing family issues is necessary for recovery. Family therapy typically begins once the patient begins putting on weight. Therapy sessions should continue even after a patient is released from the hospital. Families that value and promote thinness should be made aware of the dangerous health risks associated with anorexia and bulimia. Critical and controlling parents and siblings should become aware of how their behaviors and reactions impact the family member suffering from the eating disorder.

Drug therapy is typically used for patients with eating disorders to address depression and anxiety issues. For anorexic patients, results of drug therapy have been sporadic at best. While selective serotonin reuptake inhibitor drugs (SSRIs) are used for treating obsessive compulsive disorders, the long-term benefit has not been proven. In fact, many antidepressants often suppress the appetite. Starvation has been found to dilute the potency of antidepressants while increasing the side effects. Doctors may also prescribe cyproheptadine, an antihistamine, which often works to stimulate the appetite. Successful drug therapy for anorexic patients is very limited; a multidisciplinary approach focusing on therapy with behavior modification is most effective.

Drug therapy in conjunction with behavioral therapy has been found to be highly successful in treating persons suffering from bulimia. Anti-depressants are commonly used to address depression often found in these patients. Selective serotonin reuptake inhibitors are typically used in treating bulimics. These antidepressants are be-lieved to decrease depressive feelings and decrease the bingeing and purging cycles. Trial studies are attempting to discover if medications employed to fight drug addictions may prevent bingeing. Scientists postulate that these drugs will impede the release of opioids found in the brain during binges.

Herbs for Your Nerves

Because anorexia and bulimia are serious medical conditions, persons suffering from the disorders must seek medical help from a qualified physician and psychologist. Together, through a multidisciplinary approach (nutritionists, behaviorists, etc.), good results can be realized.

Although some herbal remedies have been successful for many people with eating disorders, taking these herbs must be done under the advisement of your doctor. Drug therapy may interact with the effectiveness of herbs or cause further health problems.

◄ Licorice Root ►

The root and juices of licorice may be used medicinally to heal stomach ulcers and calm stomach inflammation. Licorice is also suspected to help protect against viruses by promoting the manufacturing of interferon. Licorice root may also be used to improve blood sugar imbalances.

Licorice root may be taken daily. In tea, 1 to 1½ grams of crushed root may be combined with one cup of boiling water. After the water cools, the tea is ready for consumption. One-half to one gram of licorice juice, taken orally, helps sinus and throat inflammations. While 1½ to 3 grams of licorice juice can help calm ulcer pain.

Mild side effects of licorice root may result in face and ankle swelling. Licorice should not be used during pregnancy because it may induce hypertension and because high doses have been found to cause birth defects in animals. Licorice root may also reduce the effectiveness of thyroid medicine because it contains glycyrrhetinic acid, which stimulates the body's desire for thyroxin.

◄ Tahitian Noni ►

The noni fruit is the size of a potato and looks like breadfruit. The Polynesians have used the fruit for centuries as a typical food source. Ancient Polynesian writings provide information on the use of the noni fruit for medicinal and nutritional purposes throughout the ages. It is particularly useful in times of famine.

World War II soldiers discovered the fruit while based in the South Pacific islands. The noni fruit was found to increase the soldiers' strength and stamina. The noni fruit has been proven to improve strength and cell revitalization because it is a rich source of proxeronine.

◄ Spirulina ►

This wonderful blue-green microalgae has an amazingly high concentration of nutrients. Spirulina has been on Earth for over 3.5 billion years, with centuries of human consumption and over thirty years of research supporting its benefits. Besides increasing energy levels, spirulina improves our immune system, heightens natural detoxification, promotes increased cardiovascular functioning and healthy cholesterol, provides antioxidant protection against cancer, and ameliorates digestive and gastrointestinal health. Spirulina has been nicknamed the "superfood" because of its wonderful health benefits and nutritional offerings. Spirulina has the highest concentration of protein and beta-carotene. It is rich with vitamin B_{12}, iron, and ganima linolenic acid. Nutritional deficits often block the gamma linolenic acid produced in our body; thus spirulina can provide missed nutrients needed for health. Compared to other foods, spirulina crops have twenty times more protein per acre than soybeans. Spirulina boasts 200 times more protein per acre than beef. Its concentration of beta-carotene is ten times that of a carrot. Spirulina is an excellent food for vegetarians due to the high levels of protein.

Spirulina has been used to support rapid weight gain for undernourished children in West Africa. This algae has also been used with the children of Chernobyl to reduce the allergic reactions from radiation. Spirulina was also found to decrease radionucleides by 50 percent. Currently, studies are using spirulina for treating HIV-positive patients. Many infections can impede the absorption of nutrients in foods, leaving patients weak. These infections can lead to full-blown AIDS; thus, optimum strength is needed for protecting against viruses and bacteria. Japanese researchers have used spirulina in pregnant women to impede the likelihood of passing HIV-1, influenza, herpes, and mumps viruses to their unborn children.

Spirulina can be found in powder and tablet form. Scientific evidence supports the daily dose of 2 to 5 grams of spirulina. For optimum benefits, it should be taken every day. Although it is high in protein and amino acids, it has very few calories.

Quassia

Quassia is a small tree native to Brazil, Venezuela, Colombia, Argentina, and other parts of South America. There it was used to treat malaria and fevers. Additionally, it has been used as an insecticide, to treat hepatitis, and even to help treat measles.

In Brazilian medicine, it is now used as a tonic for stomach and digestive problems. Quassia helps stimulate the appetite because it helps to produce saliva and digestive juices. The bark of the quassia tree is the part used medicinally. Generally, because the quassia wood is so hard, cups made from the bark are used. Fill the cup with boiling water, allow it to cool, and drink. **Caution:** While in small doses quassia helps to stimulate the appetite, in larger doses it acts as an irritant and causes vomiting.

Holy Thistle

There are fourteen species of thistles in Great Britain alone. Thistles for the most part grow throughout Europe and Asia. For centuries, holy thistle (also known as blessed thistle) has been used for its medicinal properties. Holy thistle is a highly regarded plant; once known as a "heal-all," it was said to even cure the plague.

More recently, holy thistle has been used to stimulate appetite. It helps to produce gastric juices, thereby helping one regain appetite. To use, steep half a teaspoon of the whole herb to one pint of water for five to twenty minutes. Drink one to two cups daily.

Chapter 14
Kids

Mankind owes to the child the best it has to give . . .
—Opening words of the
United Nations' Declaration
of the Rights of the Child

Being a child does not exactly meet the requirements of a psychiatric disorder (assuming that you are under twelve). However, many people might argue that being an adolescent does. I do feel that it is appropriate to discuss herbal remedies and children. I mention later in this section that I believe that the less substances you give a child, the better, and that includes both prescribed medications as well as herbs, but sometimes you must. All children need to receive their usual course of well-baby vaccinations for several reasons. First you want to prevent the development of a physical disorder such as mumps, polio, measles, and the like. Secondly, you absolutely want to avoid some of the unfortunate problems associated with childhood disorders that can lead to damage and unwittingly cause psychological problems. And, last of all, you don't want your child infecting other kids.

This chapter will address ADD and ADHD. I will define these problems and discuss causes and treatment modalities. Further, the concentration on behavioral helpers may help parents and kids find needed relief.

Definition

Half of all referrals for child mental health outpatient services are due to Attention Deficit Disorder (ADD) and Attention Deficit Hyperactivity Disorder (ADHD). Scientists postulate that the disorder is a result of neurological dysfunction of specific neurotransmitters in the brain. The disorders are separated by the condition of hyperactivity. Characteristics of children with ADD include distractibility, poor concentration, and short attention span. Children with ADHD exhibit the same symptoms but with hyperactivity and impulsivity. These children are described as always moving and having extreme difficulty sitting still. One study examining children with the disorders in school found those with ADD were shy, socially withdrawn, nervous, and moderately popular, while those with ADHD were aggressive, guiltless, and not popular with their peers. The study indicated that both groups were unsuccessful in school academic performance.

Literature suggests that ADD and ADHD can be described as separate or conjoined disorders. More recent research is supporting the belief of ADHD as a subtype of ADD. *The Diagnostic and Statistical Manual of Mental Disorders* (DSM IV-R) references three subtypes of the disorder: the predominantly inattentive type, the predominantly hyperactive-impulsive type, and the combined type. Findings indicate that girls are more likely to qualify for the inattentive type, while boys more commonly exhibit the hyperactivity component.

Diagnosis

Teachers and parents are increasingly concerned about the success of children with ADD/ADHD in school. Because of the need to sit and listen for lengthy periods of time, children with ADD/ADHD are experiencing school failure. As a result, medicating young children has become epidemic. In diagnosing the syndrome, it is important to consider whether the child displays the characteristics at school and home. The irony of ADD/ADHD is that just as many children are overdiagnosed as those that are underdiagnosed. Remember that children by nature are rambunctious and easily excited. Boys especially display noisy and disruptive behavior, which may account for the higher number of males diagnosed with ADD/ADHD compared to females.

Diagnosis of ADD/ADHD must come from a diagnostic team of trained professionals. Team members may include a physician, psychologist, diagnostician, special educator, and behavioral therapist. Team members should address the physical, emotional, and learning difficulties commonly associated with ADD/ADHD.

Typically, a teacher may recognize problems a child is having staying focused and on task in school. A good teacher will try a variety of teaching and learning strategies to help the child before seeking further assistance. These strategies may include, but are not limited to, sitting close to the teacher, having a quiet place to work, frequent gentle cues to get back on task, and discussions with the child and parents about other techniques that may help. The teacher should be documenting the strategies and the success rates. Next, the teacher should consult a special educator for additional strategies and support ideas. If the child is not successful, the parents may consider seeking medical assistance for appropriate diagnosis and to rule out a bipolar disorder or other possible disorders.

A physician diagnosing a child will typically refer to *The Diagnostic and Statistical Manual of Mental Disorders* by the American Psychiatric Association. The manual outlines a checklist for determining if a child has ADD/ADHD. Conditions must be exhibited for six months or more and be inappropriate for a child's developmental age. The checklist asks if a child is careless to detail, has difficulty maintaining attention on tasks, has trouble with organization, is restless, has trouble remaining seated, and is unable to play quietly. Correct diagnosis requires that characteristics occur in more than one setting, that onset occur before seven years of age, that there be evidence of difficulty in social and academic performance, and that the behaviors are not the result of a developmental disorder or psychiatric problems.

Other diagnostic tools include the *Test of Variabilities of Attention* (TOVA) and the *Attention-Deficit Disorders Evaluation Scale—School Version* (ADDES-SV). The TOVA is a computerized program normed for ages four and a half to eighty. The TOVA is also used to detect learning disabilities, obsessive compulsive disorders, depression, and conduct disorders. The TOVA measures response accuracy, reaction time, and variability. A trained technician administers the TOVA in a thirty-minute session.

The ADDES-SV was developed to measure the components of ADD as asserted in the third edition of *The Diagnostic and Statistical Manual of Mental Disorders*. The test was normed on 4,876 students with ages ranging from four and a half to twenty-one. The rating scale consists of sixty items that measure three subscales: inattention, impulsivity, and hyperactivity. The ADDES-SV should be used for screening purposes, not as a single diagnostic tool.

As with all types of diagnosis, testing accuracy is dependent on the reliability and validity of the test. A single test or checklist is not appropriate for accurate diagnosis. Consultations with the child, parents, teachers, and significant adults in the child's life are necessary. A history of difficulty should be established. All possible areas of problems must be addressed before an accurate diagnosis is given.

Although many physicians are diagnosing children with ADD/ADHD, having a deeper understanding of the syndrome is necessary for accurate diagnosis. One study has suggested that teachers and parents of hard-to-control, rambunctious boys with poor grades pressure physicians into diagnosis. With structure and appropriate support, the boys could be successful without the ADD/ADHD label or the accompanying medication. Thus, finding a trained diagnostic team in the area of ADD/ADHD is imperative.

Children's hospitals or hospitals with child development units are often the first place to seek diagnosis and treatment. Universities with educational and medical schools are also a good resource.

The schools should address pediatric neurology, developmental pediatrics, and a variety of child development programs.

Causes

Although ADD/ADHD is hypothesized as a neurological dysfunction, specific causes are still under research. Familial links of ADD/ADHD are being reported. It is not uncommon for a parent to report experiencing the same difficulty remaining attentive and on task in school. Other parents report having a sibling with similar characteristics. Because of a likely genetic link, parents may be opposed to medical treatment. What is considered "normal" behavior in many households may be the result of long histories of the disorder exhibited in the family for generations.

Another interesting outcome of children being evaluated for ADD/ADHD is the parent often recognizes his/her own disorder and can be treated. Research indicates that the disorder is not cured with age but is often compensated. Many adults who experienced ADD/ADHD as children have learned coping mechanisms in order to become successful in life. ADD/ADHD in adulthood may manifest in different ways leading to depression and mood swings.

Another theory on the cause of ADD/ADHD addresses nutrient deficits in early life. Malnourishment of protein and calories during infancy and early childhood impacts anatomical and biochemical functioning of the brain. The first six months of life are particularly critical to proper nutrition. During this period of life maximal postnatal brain cell division transpires. Harm induced during this crucial time is most likely permanent. Additionally, children with a history of brain injury, brain infections, and fetal alcohol syndrome are often diagnosed with ADD/ADHD once they enter school.

Treatment

Typical treatment for ADD/ADHD is medication with stimulant drugs. The most common drug used is Ritalin (methylphenidate). Ritalin is fast-acting. Within thirty minutes a child will notice the effects. The most common dosage of Ritalin is only active for two to four hours, but it is available in a longer-acting form of 20 milligrams. Unfortunately, individuals report that the longer-lasting effect is only seven hours or less.

Dexedrine, also a stimulant drug, is slower to action than Ritalin but lasts three and a half to four and a half hours. The longer-lasting Dexedrine tablets offer relief for six to eight hours. Dexedrine is more commonly used for adolescents and adults with ADD/ADHD because of its high potency. Insurance companies are often reluctant to pay for Dexedrine because it is listed as a diet control medication. Yet, Dexedrine has been successfully helping patients curb the symptoms of ADD/ADHD for over fifty years.

Cylert is not as popular as Ritalin and Dexedrine because of cost, effectiveness, and possible interactions with other medications. Taken properly and under the care of a physician, Cylert is a successful stimulant drug for combating ADD/ADHD. Caution should be used in taking Cylert when liver or kidney dysfunctions are known or other medications are being consumed. Cylert typically takes a one- to two-week buildup period before optimum effects are felt.

Stimulant drugs are effective in controlling many symptoms of ADD/ADHD, but once the drug has worn off, the symptoms reappear. Because medication is not a panacea for ADD/ADHD, other alternatives should be investigated. Group therapy, family therapy, support groups, and behavioral therapy may help the child.

Behavioral Helpers

Group therapy provides empathy and support from other children experiencing the same difficulties. A counselor trained in the area of ADD/ADHD can offer advice and comfort as he or she leads the group discussions. An additional benefit to group therapy is that it requires children to remain focused on the discussion. The children learn from the modeling of others in the group different coping techniques for maintaining attention during the discussion. The children can then apply these strategies to other settings, such as school.

Family therapy and support groups offer support for the child with ADD/ADHD and the family members of the child. Parents and siblings are provided with a deeper understanding of the disorder and offered child management strategies. Empathy and support is given from other families in similar situations. Finally, the child with ADD/ADHD has a united front in combating the symptoms of the disorder. Because the self-esteem of children with ADD/ADHD is often poor, family counseling offers additional comfort and support.

Behavioral therapy is often useful for helping children with ADD/ADHD. Structure and routines are beneficial to impulsive and nervous children, providing predictable situations. Clear expectations are advantageous to all children, especially those experiencing behavioral difficulty.

Nutrition is another avenue of treatment that has rendered limited success. Use of vitamins and control of sugars may be suggested for treatment. Appropriate daily use of vitamins will offer health benefits, but research has indicated that it does not control ADD/ADHD symptoms. Controlling sugar intake and caffeine may offer benefits for hyperactivity, but more support in the form of medication and therapy is suggested.

School support is a major focus because of the numerous characteristics associated with the disorder. The most common of ADD and ADHD symptoms impact academic success. This is of critical concern because children spend a large amount of time in school and school-related activities. Although the federal law that requires schools to provide services to students with disabilities, the Individuals with Disabilities Education Act (IDEA), does not recognize ADD/ADHD as a disability category, services can be provided under the categories of learning disability, emotional disorder, or other health impairments. Having ADD/ADHD as an accompanying component to another disability makes sense when one considers that 20 to 40 percent of children with learning disabilities have ADD/ADHD. Additionally, 25 to 30 percent of persons with panic disorders and emotional disorders are identified as having ADD/ADHD.

An individual education plan is invaluable. Once diagnosed as having a disability under IDEA, the child is provided an Individual Education Plan (IEP) that addresses academic deficits the child is experiencing. Besides academic accommodations, the IEP can offer behavior modifications to support the child.

Token economy is one commonly used behavior modification technique. The tokens are used to reward the child for appropriate behavior and maintaining focus. Schools and teachers may be reluctant to implement the token economy system because of time requirements, financial feasibility, and fairness to other students. One way to combat this resistance is to set up the system for the teacher, alleviating the time constraints teachers often feel. Providing rewards (pencils, stickers, etc.) for all students will help abate the money and fairness issue.

Herbs for Your Nerves

ADD and ADHD, to one degree or another, involve attention, memory, inhibition, and arousal. There are broad symptoms, and so it is reasonable to worry that some kids who have been diagnosed with these disorders are possibly misdiagnosed, or the severity is inaccurately assessed. When one of the above is suspected, the child should be carefully evaluated, and psychometric testing is advised. A multidisciplinary evaluation is imperative. You want to make certain that a bipolar illness is not present. A bipolar illness, or manic depression, may often mimic the symptoms associated with ADHD. Kids who suffer from a bipolar illness will most likely need to be medicated in order to help them cope with the symptoms, but the medication for bipolar illness is different than those used for ADD and ADHD. Some children who are diagnosed with ADD or ADHD clearly would benefit from stimulant therapy, but others could be well managed through behavior modification programs, both at home and at school. It clearly is an individual call.

When it comes to medication for children, less is better. That also includes herbal remedies. Arriving at an appropriate dose for an herb is, at best, arbitrary. One author suggested that if the child is between two and twelve, give them one-quarter of the adult amount. If they're over twelve and up to the age of sixteen, give them one-half of the adult dose. This very unscientific suggestion can be quite damaging to a child.

Chapter 15
Conclusion

The universe operates through dynamic exchange—giving and receiving are different aspects of the flow of energy in the universe.

—*Deepak Chopra, M.D.*

When people come into my office, it is usually with a troubled mind and a heavy heart. They feel the weight of their pain in burdening proportions and express it openly. Rage, despair, anguish, and fear (to name a few) have become their companions. While this is not the case for most of the people that I see, it is for some.

The ribbon that ties these chapters together is alternative healing with the emphasis on herbal remedies. Contained in a cornucopia of flowers and leaves, these herbs decorate our forests, jungles, mountains, and plains. Much like the weeds we must pull from our gardens, so too must we pull the weeds that tangle the mind. But how?

If ribbons tie the chapters, then the final thought becomes the bow. One other form of alternative healing is the power of prayer. There has always been an acceptance by humankind of an almighty, omnipotent existence—God. Some may argue the nonexistence of God, but polls consistently demonstrate that about 88 percent of Americans believe that God is the source of our creation. But is God accessible? Can we ask for divine intervention?

Scientific attempts to objectively assess the efficacy of prayer have led to some very impressively designed experiments. Over the past two decades, a group of researchers have dedicated themselves to examining prayer. They have adopted the name "Spindrift," which refers to sea spray, a rather lovely visualization. The Spindrifts made certain assumptions—that all humans have a connection and oneness with God, and that God is not in a localized place, but is everywhere. In an effort to answer the question of whether spiritual healing is real or does prayer work, they constructed a simple, biologically based test. A pan containing rye seeds was divided in half, each containing equal numbers and planted under the same conditions. Half of the seeds in the pan were prayed for. A scientific study is reliable only if the results can be reproduced and are quantifiable. This study was repeated, and the rye seeds counted. The results were consistent. The half that was prayed for consistently grew more shoots than the half that was not.

Another question was asked. Would the prayed-for seeds still germinate if they were damaged or injured or unhealthy? Using the same procedure, saltwater was added to the container. Amazingly, there was an even greater growth from the damaged seeds after prayer for the seeds was added. Could this indicate that perhaps prayer is even more effective when there is trauma or things "go awry"? Apparently so. The researchers repeated the experiment and increased the amount of salt and amount of prayer each time. And each time the seeds grew more abundantly.

Switching gears, the Spindrifts repeated the experiment using soy beans, and incrementally, additional stressors were introduced. Regardless of the temperature and other variables, praying was more effective the greater the trauma. What does this mean? The more dire the situation is in life, the more positive the impact of prayer.

What about the amount of prayer given? If one prays for fifteen minutes as opposed to one hour, is the difference significant? Once again there was a positive proportionate relationship between the length of prayers and amount of germination. Another component of the effectiveness of prayer is the knowledge regarding the nature of the problem. Experiments consistently demonstrated that the more one knows about why the prayers are necessary, the greater the results. What one may ask in prayer, or how direct the praying, becomes fascinating. When praying for someone who is ill, research suggests that prayer directed toward a specific outcome, in this case a cure, is less effective than a nondirected prayer. A nondirected prayer would be modeled after the Lord's Prayer, "Thy will be done." There is no attachment to the results; rather it is left to God and the wisdom of the universe.

As compelling as the Spindrift research may be, some experiments from Redlands University in California shed even more light on the power of prayer. Researchers wanted to measure the effects of psychotherapy as compared to prayer. They selected 45 people and divided the subjects into three groups. In the first group, members were treated using classical, individual psychotherapy. The next group of subjects had no psychotherapy; instead, they relied exclusively on prayer. The third group's members would meet weekly to examine the issue of how to pray. Because the forty-five subjects all had some form of psychological issues, psychometric testing was done prior to the experiment and readministered at the end to demonstrate change, if any.

If people could identify their issues and direct their prayers accordingly, what would be the result? In the group that met to learn and discuss how to pray, members, based on their psychometric testing, were given envelopes each week that contained a specific area in their healing. The results were surprising. The second group that was told to "just pray" showed no improvement. The first group that was treated by psychotherapy showed an overall improvement by 65 percent. But the third group in which specific problem areas were paired with specific healing, a 72 percent overall improvement occurred. The conclusion was that the "prayer therapy" was the most effective way to treat psychological problems.

The flaws in this study are obvious. Even so, one cannot deny the significance of the research. The research suggested that prayer in conjunction with psychotherapy might be very useful.

Personal responsibility is at the core of psychological growth. It would be a grave injustice to God if one believed that God is the cause of the good and bad in life. Free will implicitly means a choice, and we, in our own lives, are the decision makers.

If you accept the findings of the research presented, the answer to my question, "How do we weed the tangles from our mind?" is obvious. With a sense of reverence and an abiding belief that we are truly part of divinity, prayers will be heard. Prayers must come from an honest and open mind eager to receive spiritual grace and wisdom. Attempts to manipulate the outcome prove futile and are the results of ego. Prayer is the sacred forum where man and God commune.

Our Sixth Sense

Intuition whispers to us when we least expect it. When we pray or meditate, we expect and anticipate a message; even silence speaks. But sometimes while watching children at play, listening to a friend, or just doing life's mundane chores we are suddenly aware of a gut feeling, a hunch, something tugging on our sleeve gently arousing our sixth sense.

Independent of cognition or reason, but perhaps related to a kind of *a priori* knowledge, intuition beckons you. Where a dearth of information resided, clarity now exists.

Our first five senses both protect and help create our feelings, perceptions, and moods emanating from the external forces that we call everyday living. But our sixth sense specializes in our internal realm, giving additional information to the brain acting in concert with the other five senses. This sixth sense, identified as peptide transmitters that are produced by our immune system, is what wards off mind/body stress and disease.

Logically, the more control you have over what your senses convey to your mind/body, the healthier, happier, more energetic, and peaceful you will become. Conceptually, the sixth sense is a catalyst and echoes the frontiers of the mind/body/spirit technology. This is the medical direction of the new millennium.

We are told that this phenomenon takes place on a cellular level—peptides are stored in the organs and in the mind. The gentleness of the spirit affords us the opportunity to glimpse the unknown through dreams, sensorial experience, and emotion.

Accessing Intuition

Not long ago, I was doing a segment on *Good Morning Texas* (a local TV show), discussing how to sharpen your intuitive skills. We began with a question, "Is it going to rain today?" Next, I asked the host to draw any symbol he might think of on a piece of paper. He drew several raindrops. With the question firmly in mind, I asked him to draw another symbol or picture. After some kidding around and a little "oh come on, Dr. Ann," he again drew several more raindrops. I asked him to repeat the question aloud and look at his drawing for the answer. In Todd's second drawing—the one that tweaks intuition and answers the question—he had drawn several disproportionately huge raindrops, much to his surprise. Todd's interpretation of this intuitive "art" was key. By the way, it poured all day long.

Intuition can kick in any time, anywhere, but as you have just seen, it can also be summoned. You do not need to have "psychic" abilities, just a question and a willingness to take a chance. Like a genie in a bottle, intuition can be a magical adjunct to life's conundrums. Do I think it is a panacea and should be immediately trusted? No, that would be impulsive. I do, however, believe it should be listened to.

In Tune with the Universe

The following are some helpful hints regarding this new skill:

1. Meditate regularly. A loving heart open to goodness allows you to focus your awareness.
2. Forgiveness cleanses the spirit and acts as a springboard to intuitive thought.
3. Practice, practice, practice. Whenever possible, test yourself by guessing unimportant data—which grocery line is going to open up next, is it heads or tails, and so on.
4. Keep track of your hits. See how often you are correct and record your perceptive talent.
5. Notice how your body feels when your hunch is right and make a note of it.
6. Create a sanctuary. We all need a sacred place to go and feel at one with the universe.

Postscript

It is my most profound and deepest conviction that mind and body, psyche and soma cannot be separated. What is in your mind quite literally is in your body. Acting as one incredible entity, life prospers.

Any attempt to isolate and treat just one part of you fails because it denies your total being. Based upon my years of clinical practice and supported by empirical data, I recognize that the mind/body is a wondrous creation that is limited only by us.

Tiny molecular messengers called peptides convert feelings into chemicals! This amazing link between your thoughts and your mental and physical well-being resides in the limbic/hypothalamic area of the brain. Vast clusters of receptors (in which peptides fit) trigger hormones that affect cellular activity. Remarkably, we now understand that receptors are located not just in the brain but in other parts of the body as well. Further, it is clear that your mind and body act in tandem, conversing back and forth. Our thoughts, feelings, and perceptions are the impetus that begins this process. So, why am I telling you about all this? Because your understanding of the dynamics of mind and body truly is a matter of life and death. Chemicals (thoughts) cure or kill. The key to a satisfying and healthy life requires us not only to listen to what our bodies are saying to us but what our thoughts are saying to our bodies.

Within the scientific community it is believed that the cure for many of humanity's ills, such as heart disease, diabetes, cancer, and AIDS, rests on the floor of our rain forests or the vast expanse of the Serengeti. You and I have just been on a brief exploration, a sojourn to rediscover herbs that have been known for eons. These "miracles from the garden" enchant us with their beauty, delight us with their fragrance, and soothe us in our suffering. When I began writing this book, my intention was to bring people an alternative to costly medications and to hopefully ease emotional discomfort. As I step back, I now realize that perhaps there is a better plan—that this book will provide a guide to natural medication, which can be a pathway to the psychological help that has eluded so many, chiefly because of expense.

After embarking on this enlightening path, it will indeed be difficult to walk by a plant or a blossom and dismiss it as mere vegetation. Each shrub, no matter how humble, each tree, no matter how gnarled, each flower, no matter how fragile, holds the potential to bring relief and alleviate pain. In their own way, they represent the dignity of humankind.

Appendix

How many micro and macro stressors are you feeling?

Dr. Keith Schnert modified the Holmes-Rahe Instrument in which one self-tests for stress levels. The test identifies the major and minor stressors that people may experience in life. Each event is given a numerical value. For example:

Life Event	Stress Rating
Divorce	73
Pregnancy	40

The test, based on the events in your life in the past twelve months, predicts whether you are likely to experience an illness or disease. It does not mean that it will happen, only that it is a possibility. The point of this self-test is to help you take a look at your life and change things where you can. Obviously, you cannot change the death of a spouse, but you can learn coping skills that will help to reduce the stress and pain.

Life Change Scale

Think of what has happened to you during the past twelve months. Write the point value on each line as many times as each of these events occurred during the year. Then add up your total score.

Life Event	Stress Rating	Your Score
Death of spouse	100	_____
Divorce	73	_____
Marital separation	65	_____
Jail term	63	_____
Death of close family member	63	_____
Personal injury or illness	53	_____
Marriage	50	_____
Fired from job	47	_____
Marital reconciliation	45	_____
Retirement	45	_____
Change in health of family member	44	_____
Pregnancy	40	_____
Sexual difficulties	39	_____
Gain of new family member	39	_____
Business readjustment	39	_____

Change in financial state	38	_____
Death of close friend	37	_____
Change to different line of work	36	_____
Change in number of arguments with spouse	35	_____
Mortgage over $40,000	31	_____
Foreclosure of mortgage or loan	30	_____
Change in responsibilities at work	29	_____
Son or daughter leaving home	29	_____
Trouble with in-laws	29	_____
Outstanding personal achievement	28	_____
Spouse begins or stops work	26	_____
Begin or end work	25	_____
Change in living conditions	25	_____
Revision of personal habits	24	_____
Trouble with boss	23	_____
Change in work hours or conditions	20	_____
Change in residence	20	_____
Change in schools	20	_____
Change in recreation	19	_____
Change in church activities	19	_____
Change in social activities	18	_____
Mortgage or loan less than $40,000	17	_____
Change in sleeping habits	16	_____
Change in number of family get-togethers	15	_____
Change in eating habits	15	_____
Vacation	13	_____
Christmas	12	_____
Minor violations of the law	11	_____
Your Total		_____

Your score is termed your *life-change units* (LCU). LCU is a measure of the stressors you have encountered this past year.

Interpretation of Score:

150–199 (LCU)	=	37% chance of illness or disease
200–299	=	51% chance
300 plus	=	79% chance

You have just taken an important inventory of the events that have happened to you in the last year. Now, I need you to turn your attention to what your mind and body are doing about these events.

Dr. Wildemann's Personal Stress Analysis

Directions: Look back over the past six months. Have you been noticing changes in yourself or in the world around you? Think of the office . . . the family . . . social situations. Allow about twenty seconds to reach an answer. Put a check by each part that you believe describes how you feel.

1. Do you experience any of the following physical complaints?
   ___ Overeating
   ___ Headaches
   ___ Stomach problems

- ___ Anxiety
- ___ Loss of appetite
- ___ Irritability
- ___ Muscle tension
- ___ Sadness
- ___ Cravings
- ___ Fatigue
- ___ Insomnia

2. Do you experience any of the following?
   - ___ Forgetting appointments
   - ___ Missing deadlines
   - ___ Skipping personal obligations
   - ___ Losing personal possessions (keys, glasses, and so on)

3. What about your social life? Are you:
   - ___ Seeing close friends or family members less frequently?
   - ___ Experiencing lack of enjoyment?
   - ___ Feeling overwhelmed?

4. What about time constraints? Are you too: busy to manage routine things like:
   - ___ Phone calls
   - ___ Reports
   - ___ Family gifts

5. Look at your personal life. Does sex seem like more trouble than it is worth? (0 to 3 points with zero being the least trouble)
   - ___ 0
   - ___ 1
   - ___ 2
   - ___ 3

6. What concerns you? Are you:
   ____ Second guessing yourself?
   ____ Feeling less confident?
   ____ Worried about your deadlines?
7. How about your job? Do you experience:
   ____ Conflict in your job?
   ____ Ambiguity about job expectations?
   ____ Uncertainty about your authority?

Very roughly now, place yourself on Dr. Wildemann's Personal Stress Scale. Keep in mind that this is merely an approximation of where you are and is useful as a guide on your way to a more satisfying life. Don't let a high total alarm you, but pay attention to it. My stress scale is reversible, no matter how far along you are, because it looks at you more intensely. The higher number signifies that the sooner you start being kinder to yourself, the better.

Scale Analysis

Add up each check. If you believe in God or a higher power or think of yourself as spiritual, subtract 2 points.

If your total is between:	You are experiencing:
1–6	an average amount of stress
7–19	a very high degree of stress
20+	severe threat to your physical and emotional well-being

Bibliography

Books

American Psychiatric Association, *The Diagnostic and Statistical Manual of Mental Disorders,* 4th ed. (Washington, D.C.: American Psychiatric Association, 1994).

Atkins, Robert C., M.D., *Dr. Atkins' Diet Revolution* (New York: Bantam Books Publishers, 1972).

Atkins, Robert C., M.D., *Dr. Atkins' Health Revolution* (New York: Bantam Books Publishers, 1990).

Billigmeir, Shirley, *Inner Eating* (Nashville, TN: Thomas Nelson Pub., 1993).

Bloomfield, Harold H., M.D., *Healing Anxiety with Herbs*. (New York: Harper Collins, 1998).

Blumenthal, Mark, ed., *The Complete German Commission E Monographs: Therapeutic Guide to Herbal Medicines* (Newton, MA: Integrative Medicine Communications, 1998).

Bricklin, Mark, *The Practical Encyclopedia of Natural Healing,* revised ed. (New York: Penguin Books, 1983), p. 311.

Brown, J. Donald, M.D., *Herbal Prescriptions for Better Health* (Rocklin, CA: Prima Publishing Co., 1996).

D'Adamo, Peter, M.D., *Eat Right for Your Type* (East Rutherford, NJ: Putnam Publishing Group, 1997).

Dossey, Larry, M.D., *Recovering the Soul: A Scientific and Spiritual Search* (New York: Bantam Books, 1989).

Elrod, Joe M., Ph.D., *Supplements for Fibromyalgia* (Pleasant Grove, UT: Woodland Publishing, 1998).

Hallahan, D. P., and J. M. Kauffman, *Exceptional Children,* 6th ed. (Englewood Cliffs, NJ: Prentice-Hall, 1982).

Kano, Susan, *Making Peace with Food,* revised edition (New York: Harper & Row Pub., 1989).

Kidd, Parrish M., Ph.D., *Phosphatidylsine: Number-One Brain Booster* (New Canaan, CT: Keats Publishing, Inc., 1998).

Klatz, Ronald, M.D., *Growing Young with HGH.* (New York: Harper Perennial Publishers, 1997).

Lee, William H., Ph.D., *New Power to Love* (New York: Instant Improvement, Inc., 1987).

Lerner, J., *Learning Disabilities: Theories, Diagnosis, and Teaching Strategies,* 6th ed. (Boston: Houghton Mifflin, 1993).

Lutz, R. B., and Victoria Mazies, *Herbal Medicine.* (Canyon Ranch Publication, 1999).

Michaud, Ellen, Russell Wild, et al., *Boost Your Brain Power* (New York: MJF Books, 1991).

Minirth, Dr. F. Meier, et al., *Love Hunger* (Nashville, TN: Thomas Nelson Pub., 1991).

Page, Linda R., Ph.D., *Healthy Healing* (Carmel Valley, CA: Healthy Healing Publications, 1997).

Salvia, J., and J. E. Ysseldyke, *Assessment,* 6th ed. (Boston: Houghton Mifflin, 1995).

Schnert, Keith W., M.D., *Stress Unstress* (Minneapolis, MN: Augsberg Publishing House, 1981).

Silverman, Milton, *Magic in a Bottle* (New York: The MacMillan Co., 1948).

Stoff, J. A., M.D., and C. R. Pellegrino, Ph.D., *Chronic Fatigue Syndrome* (New York: Harper Perennial, 1992).

Sullivan, Karen and C. Norman Shealy, M.D., Ph.D., *Natural Home Remedies* (Boston: Element Books Limited, 1997).

Sultenfuss, Sherry W., M.S., and Thomas J. Sultenfuss, M.D., *A Woman's Guide to Vitamins and Minerals and Alternative Healing,* revised (New York: MSF Books, 1999).

Time Life Editors, *The Alternative Advisor: The*

Complete Guide to Natural Therapies & Alternative Treatments (Alexandria, VA: Time Life Inc., 1997).

Wade, Carlson, *Natural Energy Boosters* (Upper Saddle River, NJ: Prentice Hall Press, 1993).

Walker, J. I., M.D., *Clinical Psychiatry in Primary Care* (Menlo Park, CA: Addison-Wesley Publishing Co., 1981).

Walters, Clare, *Aromatherapy: A Basic Guide* (New York: Barnes & Noble, Inc., 1998).

Weiner, M. A., Ph.D., and A. J. Weiner, *Herbs That Heal* (Mill Valley, CA: Quantum Books, 1994).

Wildemann, Ann P., Ph.D., "The Shrink Plan." (work in progress.)

Wildemann, Ann P., Ph.D., *Sessions: A Self-Help Guide Through Psychotherapy* (New York: Crossroad Publishing Co., 1996).

Worwood, V. A., *The Complete Book of Essential Oils* (Novato, CA: New World Library, 1991).

Wurtman, Judith J., Ph.D., *Managing Your Mind and Mood Through Food* (New York: Perennial List, Harper & Row Pub., 1986).

Articles

Annals of Internal Medicine, International Conference on Acquired Immunodeficiency Syndrome, November 1985, vol. 103, #5.

Bird, Luszcz, M., "Enhancing Memory Performance in Alzheimer's Disease: Acquisition Assistance and Cue Effectiveness," *Journal of Clinical Experimental Neuropsychology,* 15.

"History of Herbs," *Encyclopedia McIntosh* (Grolier Electronic Publishing, Inc., Software, 1995).

Hobbs, C., "Valerian—A Literature Review," *Herbal Gram* 21:19–34, 1989.

Holzl, J., and P. Gordon, "Receptor Binding Studies with Valeriana Officinalis on the Benzodiazapine Receptor," *Planta Med* 55, 1989.

Phillips, Anthony, Ph.D., "Memory: A Seminar," Mind Matters Seminars (Dallas, TX, November, 1999).

Rae, G. S., C. Shovlin, and K. A. Wagner, "A Double-Blind Placebo: Controlled Study of Ginkgo-Biloba Extract in Elderly Out-Patients with Mild to Moderate Memory Impairment," *Current Medical Research and Opinion*, pp. 350–355, 1991.

Smith, Lee, "What We Know About Memory," *Fortune Magazine*, April 17, 1995.

Online Sources

Advanced Herbals: *www.advancedherbals.com*
Alternative Medicine: *www.alternativemedicines.com*
American Botanical Council: *www.herbalgram.org*
A Modern Herbal Web site: *www.botanical.com*
Arthritis Foundation: *www.arthritis.org*
Biodermal Canada: *www.bio-solution.com*
Drugstore.com: *www.drugstore.com*
Esoterics: *www.oller.net*
Gardenbed: *http://gardenbed.com*

Garden Guides Web site, *www.gardenguides.com*
Health Magnets: *www.health-magnets.com*
Healthmall.com: *www.healthmall.com*
Healthy Ideas: *www.healthyideas.com*
Herbal Formulas.com: *www.herbalalternatives.com*
Herbal Information Center and Vitamin Directory: *www.kcweb.com/herb*
Herb Research Foundation's Web site: *www.ephedra.net*
JaredStory: *www.jaredstory.com*
Limited: *www.theramagnets.com*
Looksmart: *www.looksmart.com*
Louis Arkson: *www.arkson.com*
Mayo Clinic.com: *www.mayohealth.org*
Mother Nature.com: *www.mothernature.com*
National Headache Foundation: *www.headaches.org*, April 4, 2000.
Natural Land: *www.naturalland.com*
Newsweek magazine: *http://newsweek.com*
Nutri-Mart: *www.nutrimart.com*
On Health, *www.onhealth.com*
PsyCom: *www.psycome.net*
Quackwatch: *www.quackwatch.com*
Raintree Nutrition Inc.: *www.rain-tree.com/amargo.htm*
Ron Lunde's Herbs & Spices: *www.humorscope.com/herbs*
SAME-eGeneral Store: *www.samstore.com*
Spindrift Organization: *http://home.xnet.com/~spindrift/*
Symmetry International: *www.go-symmetry.com*
The Dance: *www.thedance.com*
University of Wisconsin, Madison, Department of

Botany: *www.wisc.edu/botany*
Up Country Marketing: *www.weight-free-lifestyles.com*
Vitality: *www.vitality.com*
Wampole Family Guide to Nutritional Supplements: *www.wampole.ca/english/guide.htm*
Web MD: *http://my.webmd.com*
ZiaNet: *www.zianet.com*

Index

A
AB blood type, 212
A blood type, 210–11
abuse, 85–86
"acting as if" technique, 133
acupressure, 186–87
acupuncture, 186–87
ADD. *See* Attention Deficit Disorder (ADD)
ADDES-SV. *See* Attention Deficit Disorders Evaluation Scale—School Version (ADDES-SV)
ADHD. *See* Attention Deficit Hyperactivity Disorder (ADHD)
Affective Disorders, 81, 92–93
aging, 153–71
    and behavior, 164–67
    and diet, 154–56
    and exercise, 156–57
    herbs for, 167–71
    and independence, 162–64
    and tension, 158–62
agoraphobia, 41, 49
aloe vera, 193–94
Alzheimer's disease, 118, 122, 167
amygdala, 36–37
anemone, 60–61
angelica, 24–25, 142–43
anger, 87–92, 93–95
anorexia nervosa, 223–37
    causes, 224–28
    symptoms, 231
    treatment, 228–33
antidepressants, 232–33
anxiety, 33–50

and behavior, 41–48
herbs for, 48–50
symptoms, 34–35
aphrodisiacs, 127–30, 138, 140
aromatherapy, 21–31
and aging, 171
for anxiety, 44–45
for depression, 102
for pain, 200
for skin, 22
for stress, 77, 78
arthritis, 182–84
aspirin, 122–23, 197
astragalus, 112
Atkins Diet, 208–9
atlas cedarwood, 25
Attention Deficit Disorder (ADD)
causes, 245–46
definition, 240–41
diagnosis, 241–45
treatment, 246–51
Attention Deficit Disorders Evaluation Scale—School Version (ADDES-SV), 243–44
Attention Deficit Hyperactivity Disorder (ADHD)
causes, 245–46
definition, 240–41
diagnosis, 241–45
treatment, 246–51
attitude, 160–62
Ayurvedic medicine, 4–7

B

B blood type, 211
B-complex vitamins, 154, 171
behavior modification, 19–20
and ADD/ADHD, 247–50
and aging, 164–67
and anxiety, 41–48
and Chronic Fatigue Syndrome, 108–9
and depression, 93–98
and eating disorders, 231–33
and insomnia, 57–58
and memory, 119–20
and pain, 190–92
and stress, 72–75
therapy, 248
and weight control, 212–15
belly breathing, 42–43
benzodiazapines, 48, 50
bergamot, 25–26
beta-carotene, 155
bibliotherapy, 95–96
bilberry, 147–48
biofeedback, 189–90
bipolar disorder, 81, 100, 250

bishop's hat, 135
bitter orange, 28
black cohosh, 146–47
black haw, 145
black tea, 149
blood, 9–10, 209–12
blue cohosh, 146
blue gum eucalyptus, 26
body temperature, 55–56
breathing exercises,
 42–43, 157–58
bulimia, 223–37
 causes, 224–28
 herbs for, 233–37
 symptoms, 231
 treatment, 228–33

C
caffeine, kola, 138
calcium, 177
California poppy, 49–50
capsaicin, 193
Capsella bursa-pastoris,
 147
carbohydrates, 206, 213
carotenoids, 155
Catherine the Great, 129
Caulophyllum thalictroides,
 146
caviar, 129
cayenne, 192–93
cedarwood, 25
celery seeds, 61–62
cerebral cortex, 36

chamomile, 29, 58–59
Charaka, 140
chaste tree, 143–44
Che'en Nung, 3
children, 239–51
Chinese angelica, 142–43
Chinese medicine, 4,
 7–13
chiropractic therapy, 188
chitin, 220
chlorella, 169
chocolate, 128
cholesterol, 212
choline, 171
chondroitin sulfate, 179
chromotherapy, 46–48
Chronic Fatigue
 Syndrome (CFS),
 104–14
 and behavior, 108–9
 steps to healing, 109
 symptoms, 104–7
 triggers, 107–8
Cimicifuga racemosa,
 146–47
circadian rhythm, 54–57
clary sage, 26–27
Cleopatra, 23
cluster headaches, 181–82
cognitive therapy, 45
colds, 155
color therapy, 46–48
constitutional treatments,
 6

cramping, 145
creatine, 215
Cylert, 247
Cypripedium parviflorum, 60
cyproheptadine, 233

D

D'Adamo, Peter, 210
damiana, 138–39
decision-making, 96–97
dehydro-epiandro-sterone (DHEA), 134–35, 167–68
dementia, 118, 122
depression, 79–102
   and behavior, 93–98
   causes, 80, 84–93
   and eating disorders, 227
   herbs for, 98–102
   and insomnia, 54
   and memory, 118
   and stress, 68–69
   symptoms, 82–84
desensitization, 45
Dexedrine, 246
DHEA (dehydro-epiandro-sterone), 134–35, 167–68
diabetic neuropathy, 192
The Diagnostic and Statistical Manual of Mental Disorders, 243–44
diet
   and aging, 154–56
   and sexuality, 130–31
   and weight, 207–12
Dietary Supplement Health and Education Act (DSHEA), 16
digestive problems, 144–45, 169, 194–95
disease, 68–69
Dole, Robert, 136–37
dong quai, 142–43
dopamine, 100, 140–41, 205
doshas, 4–5
drug-dependency insomnia, 53–54
drug therapy, 232–33, 246–47

E

eating disorders, 223–37
   causes, 224–28
   herbs for, 233–37
   symptoms, 231
   treatment, 228–33
Eat Right for Your Type (D'Adamo), 210
Ebers Papyrus, 3
echinacea, 110
Egyptians, 3, 23
eleuthero, 75
endorphins, 205–6
ephedra, 218–19

Epimedium grandiflorum, 135
episodic memory, 118
Epstein-Barr virus, 103–4
   herbs that inhibit, 114
   symptoms, 104–7
   triggers, 107–8
   See also Chronic Fatigue Syndrome (CFS)
erectile dysfunction (ED), 137–39
Eschscholtzia californica, 49–50
essential oils, 22–31
   uses, 24–31
eucalyptus, 26
exercise, 156–57, 214–16, 229

F

family therapy, 232, 248
fatigue, 103–14, 176
   See also Chronic Fatigue Syndrome (CFS); Epstein-Barr virus
fear, 45
feverfew, 195–96
fibromyalgia, 174–79
food, and moods, 205–7
Food and Drug Administration (FDA), 15–16
frankincense, 27

G

Gall, Franz Joseph, 116
garlic, 130
genetics, 84–85
geranium, 78
German Commission E Monograph, 17
   on chamomile, 59
   on echinacea, 110
   on ginkgo biloba, 121
   on valerian, 49
ginger root, 144–45, 194–95
ginkgo biloba, 120–21
ginseng, Asian, 112–13, 149
glucosamine sulfate, 179
glycyrrhizin, 114
golden root, 148–49
goldenseal, 178
gotu kola, 178–79
green tea, 149–50, 214
group therapy, 247
guaraná, 138
guilt, 39

H

hammamelis, 146
Han dynasty, 7, 8
HCA, 218
headaches, 179–82, 194, 195–96
heart network, 11–12
hemorrhoids, 147–48

herbs
  for aging, 167–71
  for anxiety, 48–50
  and Ayurvedic
    medicine, 6
  brands, 18
  in Chinese medicine, 7
  for depression, 98–102
  for eating disorders,
    233–37
  for fibromyalgia,
    178–79
  labeling, 16, 18
  for libido, 134–36,
    148–50
  for men, 135, 138–41
  for pain, 192–93, 200
  popularity of, 13–14
  safety of, 14–19
  for skin, 22, 193–94
  standardization of,
    14–17
  for stress, 75–78
  for weight control,
    218–21
  for women, 141–51
HGH (human growth
  hormone), 168
Hippocrates, 23
history of natural
  medicine, 1–20
HIV/AIDS, 118, 236
Holmes-Rahe
  Instrument, 263–66
honey, 128
hops, 59–60
hormone replacement
  therapy, 150–51
human growth hormone
  (HGH), 168
humor, 162
hydrotherapy, 185–86
hyperactivity. *See*
  Attention Deficit
  Hyperactivity Disorder
  (ADHD)
hypericin, 99

I

ibuprofen, 122–23
ignatia, 145
immune system, 107,
  109–14
implicit memories, 117
impotence, 137–39
independence, 162–64
Individual Education
  Plan (IEP), 249
Individuals with
  Disabilities Education
  Act (IDEA), 249
insomnia, 51–62
  and behavior, 57–58
  causes, 53–54
  herbs for, 58–62,
    170–71
intimacy anxiety,
  40–41

intuition, 258–60
iron, 155

J
jasmine, 101–2
jing, 9–10, 11
jin ye, 9–10
journals, 93–95

K
kapha, 5
kava kava, 75–76
kidney system, 11
Kleitman, Nathaniel, 52
kola, 138

L
labeling of herbs, 16, 18
lady's slipper, 60
Lashley, Karl, 116–17
lavender, 62
lecithin, 129, 171
Lee, William H., 131
lemon grass, 76–77
Lewis, Dorothy O., 91
libido, 131–36, 148–50
licorice, 113–14, 234
lifestyle, 6–7
light therapy, 93
limbic system, 21–22
lime, 27
Linnaeus, Carolus, 4
"Liquid Gold," 30, 101
liver, 10
lung network, 11
lycopene, 155

M
macular degeneration, 155
magnesium, 177
magnets, 184–85
manganese, 155
manic depression. *See* bipolar disorder
marriage, 132–34
Masters and Johnson, 131–32
M.D. Anderson Hospital and Turner Institute, 112
melatonin, 92, 170–71
memory, 115–23
  and behavior, 119–20
  herbal remedies for, 120–23
  types, 117–18
men, 138–41
menopause, 150–51
metabolism, 212–15
migraine headaches, 180–81, 195–96
minerals. *See* supplements
Ming dynasty, 7
moisture, 9
monamine oxidase, 99

Montezuma, 128
morning sickness, 144–45
motherwort, 136
motivation, 65–66, 90
Moyers, Bill, 13–14
mullein, 199–200
muscle-toning exercises, 214
music, 159–60

N

narcotics, natural, 226–27
National Center for Scientific Research, 77
nausea, 144–45, 194
neroli, 28
neurotransmitters, 84–85
New Power to Love (Lee), 131
niaouli, 28
noni, Tahitian, 234–35
nonsteroidal anti-inflammatory drugs (NSAIDS), 122–23
norepinephrine, 84, 99
NSAIDs, 122–23
nutrition, 248
See also diet
nuts, 129

O

obesity, 202–5
O blood type, 210
obsessive compulsive disorders, 39, 228
onions, 130
opioids, natural, 227
osteoarthritis, 182
oxygen, 77–78

P

pain, 173–99
   and behavior, 190–92
   herbs for, 192–200
   management, 184–90
   See also arthritis; fibromyalgia; headaches
panic attacks, 37–38, 49, 228
passion flower, 50
patchouli, 28–29
peppermint, 200
peptides, 259, 261
perception, and stress, 70–72
personalities, 4–5
pets, 74
pheromones, 24
phosphatidylserine, 121–22
pitta, 5
plant identification, 4
Pollack, Charles P., 57
poppy, 49–50
prakriti, 5
prayer, 254–58

pregnancy, 144–48
pregnenolone, 167
premenstrual syndrome (PMS), 141–44
primary depression, 81
prostate gland, 140
proteins, 206
psychodynamics, 85–87
psychotherapy, 256–57
puncture vine, 140–41

Q
qi, 8–12
quassia, 237

R
rapid eye movement, 52, 53
red clover, 178
Redlands University, 256
reishi mushroom, 111–12
relaxation techniques, 42–46
remote memory, 117
REM (rapid eye movement), 52, 53
rheumatoid arthritis, 183
Ritalin (methylphenidate), 246
roman chamomile, 29
rosewood, 29–30
royal jelly, 128–29, 169–70

S
S-Adenosylmethionine, 100
sage, 26–27
salicylic acid, 197
SAM-e, 100
sandalwood, 30, 101
sarsaparilla, 139
saw palmetto, 140
schizandra, 219–20
Schnert, Keith, 64, 263
schools, 248–49
Scutellaria baicalensis, 148–49
Seasonal Affective Disorder (SAD), 92–93, 227–28
seaweed, 169
seeds, 129
selective serotonin reuptake inhibitor drugs (SSRIs), 232–33
self-examination, 42
self-help books, 96
self-sabotage, 97–98
semantic memory, 117
sensate focus, 131–32
serotonin
  and depression, 84, 100
  and diet, 205
  and eating disorders, 227
sexuality, 125–51
  and diet, 130–31

herbs for, 128–30, 134–41, 148–49
shen, 9–10
shepherd's purse, 147
Simonten, Karl, 160
sixth sense, 258–60
skin, 22, 193–94
sleep disorders, 176
See also insomnia
sleep progression plan, 57
social anxiety, 41
Spindrifts, 254–55
spirulina, 235–36
spleen, 10–11
SSRIs (selective serotonin reuptake inhibitor drugs), 232–33
St. Johnswort, 98–100
standardization of herbs, 14–17
stress, 62–78
  and behavior, 72–75
  causes of, 65–72
  and disease, 68–69
  herbs for, 75–78
  and insomnia, 54
  measurement, 264–68
  as motivation, 65–66
stressors, 66–68
substance abuse, 118
sun, 213
supplements
  and aging, 154–56
  and pain, 177, 192
  and sexuality, 130
  and weight control, 220–21
  See also vitamins
support groups, 248
support system, 73, 95

T

teas, herbal, 149–50, 214
tension, 158–62, 180
Test of Variabilities of Attention (TOVA), 243
testosterone, 132, 135, 139, 141
therapeutic treatments, 6
See also specific therapies
thistle, holy, 237
token economy, 249–50
TOVA *(Test of Variabilities of Attention)*, 243
tranquilizers, 48, 50
trauma, 107, 112
The Treatise on Diseases Caused by Cold Factors, 7
Tribulus terresteris, 140–41
turmeric, 110–11

V

valerian, 48–49, 60, 76
vata, 5

Viburnum prunifolium, 145
vitamin C, 155, 192
vitamin E, 155
vitamin O, 77–78
vitamins
   and aging, 154–56
   and pain, 177, 192
   and sexuality, 130
   and stress, 77–78
   and weight control, 220–21

W

weight control, 201–21
   and behavior, 212–15
   diets, 207–12
   herbs for, 218–21
   supplements for, 220–21
   tips, 217–18
white willow, 196–97
wintergreen, 197–98
women, 141–51
working memory, 117–18
World Health Organization, 13
worry, managing, 158–62
"worse case scenario" therapy, 46

X

xue (blood), 9–10

Y

yams, wild, 134
yang, 8, 12
yarrow, 30–31, 198–99
ye, 9–10
Yellow Emperor, 8
yin, 8, 12
ylang-ylang, 31
yohimbe, 139

Z

zinc, 155–56

About the Author

Dr. Ann Patterson Wildemann is a recognized expert in the fields of mental health and business science. Many of you will recognize "Dr. Ann" from her years of television appearances. She has been the host of her own TV and radio programs and produced three children's programs dealing with drugs, suicide, and latchkey kids. Currently she is a regular contributor to *Good Morning Texas* on WFAA, an ABC network affiliate in Dallas, Texas.

Academically, Dr. Wildemann holds a B.A. and M.S., and received a Ph.D. degree from Texas Woman's University. She has been a professor in the graduate school at the University of Texas, a consultant in the Human Resource Center for the state of Texas, as well as a consultant for Project Child Find. In addition, she has authored four books.

Dr. Wildemann's warmth and humor have enhanced her demand as a speaker and seminar leader. She practices in Dallas and Arlington, Texas, where she focuses on personal development.

You may contact Dr. Wildemann at:
1615 W. Abrams Street, Suite 200I
Arlington, TX 76013
(817) 261-7290
or online at: *awildemann@msn.com*